NORFOLK RED:

The Life of Wilf Page, Countryside Communist

Dedicated to *Daily Worker/Morning Star* reporters

Arthur Milligan (1935-2001)

Les Mitchell (1938-1989)

and photographer Ernie Greenwood (1927-2009)

Note: The Norfolk Red, pictured on the previous page, was a bull renowned for its strength.

NORFOLK RED:

The Life of Wilf Page,
Countryside Communist

Mike Pentelow

Lawrence & Wishart
LONDON 2009

Lawrence and Wishart Limited
99a Wallis Road
London
E9 5LN

First published 2009

Copyright © Mike Pentelow 2009

British Library Cataloguing in Publication Data.
A catalogue record for this book is available from the British Library
ISBN 9781905007974

Text setting E-type, Liverpool
Printed and bound by Imprintdigital, Exeter

Contents

Acknowledgements

The late Peter Kentfield (1926-2006) had been writing Wilf Page's biography for some years before he died. After his death his drafts and notes were passed on, and they form the basic structure of the first five chapters of this book.

Peter had been very active in writing for the *East Anglian Pensioner* newspaper, through which he met Wilf. He had also been very active in the Communist Party, the Campaign for Nuclear Disarmament, and the peace and pensioners' movements. Born in Croydon, Peter did his army national service in the medical corps in Belfast after his application to be a conscientious objector had been rejected. On being demobbed he had several jobs before becoming a social worker in Tower Hamlets where he was involved in the strike of 1978-9 after which he left to take a history degree. While working as a locum social worker in Lewisham he met Jean, his team leader, whom he later married. They moved to Cornwall for seven years where they were very active in the peace and environmental movement – Peter being arrested for occupying a tin mine to prevent nuclear waste being dumped there. Peter and Jean came to live in Norwich in 1994, and met Wilf at a Burston rally.

From 1996 to 1998 Peter taped a total of ten hours of Wilf's reminiscences. He then taped a further 28 hours of interviews with people who had known Wilf – his daughter Carol Lorac,

Joan Maynard, Mike Ward, Helen Dunman, Ron Borrett, Ian Gibson, Ray Bunting, Barbara Smith, Chris Kaufman, Francis Beckett, George Barnard, Rev Ron O'Toole, Betty Gooch, Daphne Oliver, Arthur Amis, Peter Medhurst, Barbara Stevenson, and Len Stevenson.

A further five hours of Wilf's memories of his life in India with the RAF were taped by Conrad Woods, a sound recordist with the Imperial War Museum, who was also a Communist Party member from Bury St Edmunds. RAF Cranwell in Sleaford, Lincolnshire, was able to provide brief details of Wilf's service record. Another invaluable source was the 25,000 words of Wilf's recollections which were earlier recorded and transcribed by Alan Duvet. Additional personal memories were supplied to me by Carol Lorac, Wilf's close friend Mike Ward, *Landworker* ex-editors Francis Beckett and Chris Kaufman, Peter Melchett and Peter Medhurst.

Much material and old *Country Standards* were supplied by Tony Gould. The Marx Memorial Library were also very helpful in looking up back issues of a number of periodicals and other documents. Peter McShane at the Museum of English Rural Life (University of Reading) was most helpful in making its archives available. Liz Hurrell, headteacher of Horsham St Faith School, provided information about the school. Nigel Morter, principal lecturer in Labour and Trade Union Studies at London Metropolitan University, provided information on army and airforce education. Information about the Norfolk Red bull was supplied by Paula Mayfield of the Rare Breeds Survival Trust. Apart from the books listed in the bibliography, other written sources that were most useful were the *Eastern Daily Press*, *North Norfolk News*, *Daily Worker*, *Morning Star* and *Landworker*.

Peter Everard Smith provided many photographs of Wilf in

the last twenty years of his life. The cartoons were drawn by Chris Tyler. The woodcut illustrations were by Clifford Harper. David Turner helped scan the illustrations and checked the copy.

Introduction

Wilf Page was a widely respected giant of the national and international trade union movement, a promoter of justice in the countryside, a communist councillor during the difficult cold war years and a lifelong community activist. He has recently been likened to his contemporary Nelson Mandela, on the grounds that he never became bitter about the discrimination he suffered because of his political beliefs. He accepted it as the price that had to be paid for the cause of progress. Instead of being dejected by discrimination – which affected him particularly in his search for work as a young father – it merely strengthened his resolve to abolish the unjust social system which spawned it.

Page is Norfolk dialect for an assistant shepherd, yet this seems to be one of the few jobs Wilf did not try his hand at. Blacklisted by employers because of his trade union activities, he had to scrape a living from a string of short-term jobs. He could have been a guest almost every week on the 1950s television programme *What's My Line* (in which a panel had to guess the occupation of guests from a mime). In his early days he had been a rag and bone man, a servant, an upholstery apprentice, a barman, a ballroom dancer-cum-gigolo, and a potato picker, before becoming an aerial photographer for the Royal Air Force in India. After the war he was a Labour Party agent, beach photographer, cafe manager, lorry driver, bus driver, gardener, caravan site attendant, travelling fish salesman, and occasional farmworker.

Perseverance was one of his qualities, and he kept plugging away against right-wing opposition in his union, the National Union of Agricultural Workers, finally being elected to its executive after seventeen years of standing. Once elected, his talent was officially appreciated and, when the union later merged with the Transport & General Workers' Union, he served on its executive, representing agricultural and rural workers. As he became recognised as an elder statesman of the union, he was elected as president of the European Federation of Agricultural Unions.

In all these prestigious positions he was well known for his communist views. But his honesty and integrity won him respect, even from those who vehemently opposed his politics. And it was this, coupled with his record of getting things done – both through official channels and more unorthodox means – which led to him being returned as a communist councillor time and again in Edgefield, Norfolk, during twenty-eight of the worst years of the cold war.

Wilf's humour and fortitude enabled him to come through many trying times – from being punished for organising a strike at school, to burying his own grandfather in a macabre do-it-yourself funeral, to being arrested and fined for cutting a wire fence around a US nuclear base. Even when, towards the end of his life, he saw the collapse of the Soviet Union and the other socialist countries, he did not see it as a reason to give up hope. Instead he drew a positive lesson, that communists should think more for themselves instead of accepting things without question as they had done in the past. He saw marxism not as a dogma but as a way of analysing society and the forces within it, as an essential part of the battle for social justice.

On his death, an obituary in *The Times* accurately reported that Wilf's communism had not been of the 'big Russian bear' variety, but had been about 'the community owning the wealth'. He was a man whose tireless battle for justice lasted until the last day of his life.

1. Norfolk's labour heritage

Wilf Page was born shortly before the outbreak of the first world war in a tiny cottage in Newton St Faith, just north of Norwich, where his father was a rag and bone man. His mother had been a domestic servant. His destiny was to continue a long Norfolk tradition of working-class struggle, and to become the leading agricultural trade unionist in Europe. This first chapter outlines Wilf's heritage – the rich history of the struggles of the rural workers of Norfolk.

The peasants' revolt in Norfolk

That tradition of rural struggle in Norfolk goes back at least to 1381, when Geoffrey Litster, a dyer from Felmingham, near North Walsham, led the peasants' revolt against the poll tax in Norfolk. He and his fifty thousand men pillaged the houses of nobles, lawyers and other wealthy individuals, before entering Norwich and occupying the castle. Here he forced knights to wait upon him on their knees – to show what it was like to be on the receiving end of feudal servitude.

To demonstrate their break with the authority of the church, the rebels went to Carrow Priory, to seize all the deeds and court rolls and take them back to the centre of Norwich and publicly burn them. This upset the Bishop of Norwich, Henry Despenser – trained as a soldier and described as a warrior bishop. He mustered a large army to attack the rebels, who then retreated to North Walsham, digging in behind barricades made from tables, carts, doors and other furniture. These were easily overcome by the professional soldiers and Litster was captured. Some of his followers fled for sanctuary to a church that was under construction, but the bishop knew it had not yet been consecrated, and no religious scruple prevented him from entering the church and hacking them all to death.

The bishop then granted Litster absolution, and ordered him to be hung, drawn and quartered. This meant that Litster was hanged slowly in order to prolong the agony (without a sudden drop), cut down while still conscious, disembowelled, forced to watch his own entrails being burned in front of him, before finally being beheaded. His torso was cut into four parts, which were suspended in different places – at his own home, at one of the city gates in Norwich, at Kings Lynn, and at Great Yarmouth.

Kett's rebellion

Wymondham, where Wilf was baptised, and where he lived for some years, was also the town where Robert Kett (1492-1549), a tanner, had once lived. In 1549 Kett led a rebel army of twenty thousand farm labourers against landowners who had been fencing off common land – land on which smallholders and others depended for the grazing of their animals. There had been earlier Norfolk riots against the enclosures – at Fakenham in 1520 and 1525, Walsingham in 1537, Hingham in 1539, Griston in 1540, Great Dunham in 1544, and Great Yarmouth, Middleton and King's Lynn in 1548. But they all had failed through lack of leadership.

This missing ingredient was provided by Kett in 1549. After he addressed a crowd from an oak tree ('Kett's Oak', a subsequent tree, still grows on the site, just south of Hethersett on the B1172), they responded to his call to smash down the fences. The numbers swelled and the revolt spread, partly in response to his call to free all bonded men. A server in the local church, Kett had argued that God created all men free (echoing the sentiments of John Ball's sermon during the 1381 peasants' revolt). The rebels marched towards Norwich, and when they reached Easton, to the south west of the city, they sought permission to carry on to set up camp at Mousehold Heath, on the hills slightly to the north of the city. They declared: 'What we want is liberty, and the power, in common with our so called superiors, of enjoying the gifts of nature.' The city councillors refused them permission, but undeterred they carried on to the heath. In the centre of the camp they set up was a large oak tree (a Water Tower now stands there). This became known as the Oak of Reformation, and from under it Kett held councils, administered justice, issued edicts, and even appointed twenty-five governors for the surrounding areas of Norfolk and Suffolk. The rebels drew up a list of twenty-nine complaints, mainly against economic exploitation and the overbearing attitude of the lords of the manors. The document also included the phrase: 'We pray that all bond men may be made free'. The rebel army also commandeered contributions from the gentry to support them – three thousand bullocks, twenty thousand sheep, and immense quantities of corn, geese, swans and other foods. This enabled them to survive for seven weeks, with the provisions being shared out publicly under the Oak of Reformation. Members of the gentry were put on trial for enclosing the land, but were imprisoned as punishment rather than hanged.

An attack by an army of 1400 men, led by the Marquis of Northampton, was routed by the rebels, who subsequently locked up the mayor and other nobles in the Guildhall. But a much larger army of 12,000 soldiers was then sent by the king, led by the Earl of Warwick (and supported by an extra 1200 Swiss, German, Italian and Dutch mercenaries). Warwick's troops, though temporarily repulsed, soon retook the centre of the city, forcing the rebels to retreat to Mousehold Heath, and then further east to Dussindale, an outlying village. The trained royal soldiers, many of them on horseback, now broke through and slaughtered three thousand of the rebels. Of those captured, three hundred were hanged – some from the Oak of Reformation, others on the Market Cross in Norwich. Kett and his brother William, a butcher, were taken to London and locked up in the Tower, where they were put on trial for high treason and sentenced to death. Robert was hanged from a gibbet on top of Norwich Castle, and William from the steeple of Wymondham church. Their bodies remained hanging in chains for many months afterwards.

The revolt was not completely in vain however. The city corporation did move to make some concessions to offset further unrest, by ordering the wealthier inhabitants of Norwich to provide corn for the poor.

In 1949 a plaque at the entrance to Norwich Castle was erected, honouring Kett as 'a noble and courageous leader', for his part 'in the long struggle of the common people of England to escape from a servile life into the freedom of just conditions'. Kett's Tavern also stands in his memory in the city, in Kett's Hill, which leads to Mousehold Heath. The town

A portrait of Kett on the sign of the pub named after him in Norwich
© *Peter Everard Smith*

sign of Wymondham also commemorates the revolt, and a pub and a school there are named after Kett. His actions were also celebrated in a play by G. Colman Green, 'Kett the Tanner'. This was written in 1909, just four years before Wilf's birth.

Thomas Paine

Thomas Paine (1737-1809), perhaps the most famous of all international revolutionaries, was born in Thetford in Norfolk; he worked there as a staymaker, and also in nearby Diss. Paine fought for the creation of the American republic in 1777 (drafting its declaration of independence from Britain), and in the French revolution of 1789. Back in England he wrote *The Rights of Man* in support of the revolution. In 1792 he was found guilty, in his absence, of sedition, which carried the death sentence, but by then he had fled to France, where his disapproval of the intolerance of religion led to him being once more sentenced to death, in 1794 (which he evaded because the jailer chalked the death mark in the wrong place).

Although it is commonly believed that Paine was an atheist,

he was in fact a theist (believing in God but not churches, which he considered to be human inventions for enslaving mankind). In his twenties he had become a Methodist lay preacher after hearing John Wesley in Thetford, and just before his death in great poverty in America he asked to be buried on Quaker ground (a request which was refused).

Nineteenth-century rural struggles

The Captain Swing agricultural riots swept through the south east and East Anglia from 1830, and were particularly strong in Norfolk. The spark of this unrest was the introduction of labour-saving threshing machines, each of which put ten men out of work, at a time when unemployment was high and there was great poverty in the countryside. Captain Swing was the name signed at the end of letters to rich farmers demanding they grant pay rises and stop using the threshing machines. If the warning was ignored the rioters destroyed the hated machines and set ablaze farms and hayricks.

The first riots and acts of arson by agricultural labourers in Norfolk started in October 1830, and by the end of the next month they were taking place almost daily in all parts of the county (including an incident in Reepham, when rioters dragged a magistrate from his horse, and attacked firemen to prevent them putting out the fires, despite the presence of soldiers). They continued at a regular rate for the next two years – and spasmodically after that into the 1840s.

There was significant support for the agricultural workers from their fellow workers in the towns. In fact the first man in Norfolk to be executed for his part in the struggle (for setting fire to farms in the village of Swanton Abbot, ten miles north of Norwich) was Richard Nockolds (1796-1831), a hand-loom weaver from Norwich. Nockolds was an active member of the militant Norwich Weavers Society, which had been in dispute with the cloth manufacturers since 1829. The manufacturers operated by selling yarn to self-employed weavers, and then buying back the finished cloth once it had been woven in weavers' homes. In 1829 they had made drastic cuts in the price they paid to the weavers – driving many of them to apply for poor relief. The Society was against accepting the cut rate, and many of its members attacked the looms of those that did accept it. A decision by the authorities to put sixty looms into local workhouses, so that the paupers could be put to work at weaving, was seen as a move to further drive down wages. The weavers responded by blocking the delivery of the looms, and throwing them all in the River Wensum – despite troops being called in to prevent them.

Nockolds believed in education, to explain that all workers, in both town and country, shared a common class interest; and he also believed in direct action against employers who were driving down wages. Such action included throwing acid at them, and he was also present when one received a gunshot wound. Self-educated, Nockolds organised a Sunday reading club, where members paid one penny a week to buy radical literature and then read it in meetings at home – while others were attending church services. They read articles by radicals such as William Cobbett and Richard Carlile. Cobbett was a self-educated farm labourer who went on to become a leading journalist campaigning for parliamentary reform. In 1832 he was elected as a radical MP for Oldham, and demanded universal suffrage and the relief of agricultural distress (on his horseback rides around the country he concluded that farm labourers produced about fifteen times as much food as they were able to buy on their near starvation wages). In March 1830 he addressed a Norwich meeting that was attended by Nockolds. Carlile, a keen disciple of Thomas Paine, was a bookseller who was jailed for publishing pamphlets 'calculated to excite sedition and rebellion'.

In January 1831 Nockolds met Josiah Davidson of Swanton Abbot, who was trying to eke a living there both as an agricultural labourer and as a weaver. He used to walk the ten miles to Norwich and back to fetch his yarn and deliver his cloth. The two men discussed the troubles of the agricultural workers, and Nockolds enquired of Davidson whether there had been any fires in his area. On hearing that there had not been any, he offered to help. The next day Nockolds and Davidson's brother Robert set out for Swanton Abbot, where they set fire to three farms and left threatening notes at three others.

In March 1831 four men were tried for these offences – Nockolds, Josiah and Robert Davidson, and Robert Hunt. In order to save himself from the death sentence, Robert Davidson gave King's evidence against the others. Nockolds, who, unusually for a workingman in those times, defended himself (and did so confidently and articulately), was singled out for hanging, but this only served to confirm his reputation as a popular hero. Huge numbers attended his execution at Norwich Castle on 2 April 1831, and, unusually for such an event, the crowd maintained a complete and respectful silence. Hundreds paid a penny each to his widow to view his body on display outside their home, before he was buried at St James's church.

The execution had no deterrent effect, however, and the Swing riots continued. In the same month as Nockolds was hanged, Robert Davidson's own wife was arrested for making 'balls for firing stacks'. Another Norfolk rioter to hang was James Clarke of Buxton, aged just 20. He was hanged in 1835 for setting fire to a haystack on a local farm. When the judge donned the black cap, as was customary he intoned that he hoped that the Lord would have mercy on Clarke's soul. Young Clarke replied: 'Yes, there ain't much mercy on earth'. Nockolds and Clarke were two of the nineteen rioters that were hanged throughout the country; a further 481 people were transported to Australia for a minimum of seven years, most of them never to see their families again.

In spite of this savage suppression, once again the battles did wring some concessions. Wages were increased and the threshing machines were not finally replaced for a further twenty years. And the radical tradition was continued when a strong Chartist movement grew up in Norwich in the 1830s, demanding political reforms including votes for working-class men. This was part of a countrywide surge in radicalism and the beginnings of rural trade unionism during this period, which included the famous Tolpuddle Martyrs' attempts to form an agricultural union to resist wage cuts. The Tolpuddle Martyrs were transported to Australia in punishment for their activities, but were released within a few years after mass demonstrations and pressure on the government.

As well as the trial of the Tolpuddle farm workers, 1834 saw the introduction of the Poor Law Amendment Act, with all its disastrous consequences for the poor – and this led to more riots in Norfolk and elsewhere. The new law abolished outdoor relief (whereby money, coal, clothes and shoes could be distributed to the needy in their own homes) and replaced it with the workhouse system, whereby needy families were sent to the workhouse as a condition of receiving even minimal aid – and were split up and forced to live on near-starvation diets in the most cruel conditions.

Inmates at the workhouse in Edgefield (the village that would later be represented by Wilf on the local council) were among the first to rebel against this regime – by setting fire to the roof. Other workhouses to be set alight by the inmates in Norfolk included those at Heckingam, Rollesby and Long Stratton, while all the windows were smashed at Swainsthorpe. Chairs and tables were also smashed at St Faiths workhouse during a riot in 1846. (Wilf used to pass by St Faiths workhouse on his way to school, and it was also the place where his funeral was held – after it had become a crematorium.)

Another attack on the rural poor was the continuing enclosure of common land – on which they had previously been able to shoot rabbits for food, and from where they had collected wood for their fires. The villagers of Horsham St Faith were prominent in resisting this attack on their ancient rights in 1868, when during dawn raids they hacked down trees in the newly enclosed woods. Similar action had also been taken at Snettisham in North Norfolk. And in Fakenham, four protesters against the further enclosure of common land were brought before the court and charged with damaging fences that had been erected in 1870. (Many years later Wilf also appeared before a Fakenham magistrate, also charged with damaging a fence, though this time the fence in question was surrounding a nearby US air-force base.)

Rural workers increasingly found themselves being prosecuted for poaching, in areas where they had previously been free to shoot rabbits. Edgefield had a particularly high prosecution rate, but the 'poachers' remained undeterred, considering the law unjust.

Joseph Arch and the agricultural workers' union

This attitude to poaching was voiced in 1872 by Joseph Arch (1826-1919), founder of the first national agricultural workers' union. Arch declared that hares and rabbits 'were the fair property of anybody who can take them'. A staunch primitive methodist, he cited biblical support for this view – Genesis Chapter 1, Verse 26, which let men have dominion over fish in the sea, fowl in the air, and every creeping thing on earth. Arch became MP for North West Norfolk in 1885, the first ever agricultural worker to sit in parliament. Though he was voted out the following year, he was then re-elected in 1892, and represented the constituency until 1900.

On leaving school at the age of nine, Joseph had started work as a crow-scarer, and his couple of shillings a week had soon become vital to the family. His father had been blacklisted from work by farmers, because he refused to sign their petition in favour of the Corn Laws (which kept up the price of corn, and so food, by restricting imports). His mother had to take in washing to save the family from starvation. Joseph became a ploughboy at ten, and then a stable boy. When his request for a pay rise to support his family was rejected out of hand, he became a jobbing labourer, a 'freelancer', and was much in demand, especially as a hedgecutter. Because he was not dependent on a single employer he was less vulnerable than other organisers to immediate victimisation. This, as well as the public speaking skills he had learned as a preacher, made him the natural choice to lead a new union when it was set up at Wellesbourne, Warwickshire, in 1872.

Addressing the first meeting of the union, on an old pig stool on the village green, under a chestnut tree, Arch's rousing rhetoric had an immediate effect; three hundred signed up on the spot. 'I knew that a fire had been kindled which would catch on, and spread, and run abroad like sparks in stubble,' he wrote in his autobiography. 'And I felt certain that this night we had set light to a beacon which would prove a rallying point for the agricultural labourers throughout the country.' And so it proved to be.

Successful strikes won pay rises, and within two years the union had become the National Agricultural Labourers' Union, which, with over 86,000 members, was the largest union in the country.

Union pressure to extend the vote in general elections to male farmworkers finally succeeded in 1884 (seventeen years after it had been won for male town workers). This no doubt contributed to Arch's election. He was elected as a Liberal (the Labour Party had not yet been formed) and his maiden speech in the House of Commons called for radical land reform. He argued that because there was so much uncultivated land and so many unemployed agricultural workers, parliament should consider 'every legitimate means to bring the land that cries for labour to the labourers as soon as possible'.

At several conferences of the Trades Union Congress, Arch called for heavy taxation on landowners who left their land uncultivated. And he told Liberal prime minister William Gladstone that if the land were 'made free from the feudal fetters that bind it', and labour was emancipated, it would prevent future agricultural depressions. However, a series of bad harvests, droughts, and lockouts of union members finally led to the union's dissolving in 1896.

George Edwards

Just ten years later there was a revival of activity in Norfolk, which led once more to the growth of a national union. This time it was spearheaded by George Edwards (1850-1933), who had been a member of Arch's union – and had been evicted from his tied cottage as a result. Like Arch, Edwards's father was an agricultural worker who had been blacklisted by farmers, in his case for speaking out against workers' sufferings at a public meeting. He had later been jailed for stealing a few turnips to feed his six starving children, which had led to the family being broken up and sent to the workhouse. Again like Arch, young George was a primitive methodist preacher.

In 1906 the Liberals won the general election and Labour increased its number of seats to thirty as the Conservatives were routed. The Norfolk farmers took their revenge by sacking and evicting scores of workers whom they suspected of voting against the Tories. The need to organise to resist these attacks became clear, and farmworkers approached Edwards to defend them. Edwards was by then a councillor on Erpingham Rural District Council (where Wilf was to serve many years later). During his time in office Edwards had been instrumental in getting the first council houses built at Edgefield, and he had also served on the workhouse board of guardians, doing what he could to make the Poor Law administration less cruel.

Edwards hired the Angel Inn at North Walsham for a meeting, and this led to the formation of the Eastern Counties Agricultural Labourers' and Small Holders' Union, with just 122 members. Edwards became the fledgling union's secretary, with its first office a tiny bedroom in his cottage at Gresham, near Cromer (where Wilf was to end his days).

The first major victory came in 1910 at the village of Trunch (where Wilf was later to be branch chairman). The members there refused to accept an increase in the working day to ten hours, unless they got an extra shilling a week. As result they were locked out from seven farms and replaced by non-unionists (despite a pledge not to do so from Sheringham Farmers' Federation). The breaking of this promise put the men in fighting mood and they stood out against the farmers' demands, with the full support of the union. The newly recruited non-union labour was now being paid ten shillings a week more than the amount the union had been seeking, as well as getting free housing and food. But the union rallied so much support that it was able to provide generous strike pay. The Norwich branch of the Independent Labour Party also came out in support of the strikers (who included Walter Smith, later to become president of the union). After a few weeks all the farmers except one agreed to keep the hours down to nine a day. As for the one that refused: his farm was taken over by Norfolk County Council (after Edwards had used his influence as a member of the County Council's Small Holdings Committee), and was subsequently re-let in small holdings to the strikers.

Later in 1910 union members demanded an extra shilling a week and Saturday afternoons off at St Faith's (a sub-district covering the villages of Newton St Faith, where Wilf was born, and Horsham St Faith where he attended school). The farmers refused to negotiate and a dispute began. Mounted police were then brought in to escort non-union strikebreakers to the farms. But the whole village supported the strikers, and their strike pay was again boosted by factory collections in nearby Norwich. The strike lasted an incredible eight months, and was ended by only the narrowest of votes (1,102 to 1,053) – with members returning to work at the old conditions but with guarantees of no victimisation.

George retired as general secretary of the union in 1913, by which time it had grown into the National Agricultural Labourers' and Rural Workers' Union, with 12,000 members in 26 counties throughout England and Wales. By 1918 it had mushroomed further to 170,000 members, enabling it to move its headquarters from Fakenham (where George Edwards was later buried) to London. In the following year the union set up its monthly newspaper *Landworker*.

In 1920 George was elected as Labour MP for South Norfolk. Three years later he was co-opted on to the union's disputes committee to organise their rolling general strike, in which up to

10,000 farm workers at a time were called out to resist cuts in wages that brought them below the cost of living. (Wilf witnessed this strike in his village as a schoolboy.) Weekly pay had been cut from 46 to 28 shillings in the previous two years, and now the farmers were cutting it by a further two shillings and sixpence (and increasing the hours to 54 a week). Even the farmers admitted this was not enough to live on, and had asked Andrew Bonar Law's Conservative government to provide financial support to 'protect the agricultural workers from further wage reductions'. On the rejection of this request the cuts were nevertheless imposed. Further insult was added to injury when the farmers started to pay workers by the hour rather than the week, which meant they could be laid off without notice at any time of the day.

In 1924, after a long and bitter dispute, James Ramsay MacDonald (leader of the Labour Party minority government that was now in office) was called in to mediate. He got the two sides to agree to 25 shillings for a guaranteed 50 hour week, with no victimisation of the strikers. MacDonald condemned the farmers' subsequent refusal to take back 1200 of the strikers as 'a most atrocious example of dishonourable conduct' – but said there was nothing he could do about it. The strike did, however, end the imposition of wage cuts and longer working hours; and it led to the passing of the Agricultural Wages Act the following year, which provided for the setting of legal minimum pay.

In later life, Wilf was instrumental in getting a plaque erected in North Walsham to commemorate the formation of the union by George Edwards.

The Burston School Strike

In 1913 in Burston, South Norfolk, the squirearchy and farmers who controlled the parish council and school management committee were taken on by the village school's two teachers. These were Tom Higdon (1869-1939), who had become a branch secretary of George Edwards's agricultural workers' union the year after it was formed, and his wife Annie 'Kitty' Schollick (1864-1946).

Tom and Kitty had got up the noses of the local farmers by activities such as objecting to their pupils being taken out of school to work in the fields during harvest time. They had also complained that the parish council was not building cottages for farm workers, who were living in overcrowded hovels. By contrast the chairman of the council, Rev Charles Tucker Eland, who was also the vicar, had a house with twenty rooms in it for his family of three. Higdon, alongside other villagers, decided to stand for the 1913 election to the parish council, and together they swept away all but one of the sitting councillors. To rub salt in the wound, Tom came top of the poll with thirty-one votes, while the vicar was bottom with just nine. Vengeance was a strong component of the vicar's brand of Christianity, and he rapidly gained it now, by getting the Higdons sacked on the trumped up charge that Kitty had caned one of the pupils (for which no evidence was ever provided at the later enquiry).

On the day that the Higdons were evicted from the school, 1 April 1914, the pupils walked out, in a remarkably inspirational demonstration of solidarity. They marched round the village holding banners demanding the reinstatement of their teachers, and their parents also rallied in support, supplying them with food and materials to enable them to carry on teaching the children unofficially, on the village green. As the trade union movement throughout the country added their support to the cause, the case received national and international publicity, which highlighted the injustice of the sackings. Enough money was raised to build an alternative school building – known as the Burston Strike School – and this was successfully run by the Higdons until Tom's death in 1939.

When Wilf organised his own school strike in Horsham St Faith in 1923 he was not aware of the well-known strike that had taken place just twenty miles away when he had been a baby. But in his later years he helped get the Burston Strike School restored, as a memorial to this historic struggle. In 1984 he organised a rally to celebrate the school – which has been an annual event ever since – and he was a trustee of the school until his death.

2. Early days

Though Wilf's life would be part of this long Norfolk tradition of collective action, there was no history of activism in his family. His father Billy had formed an early aversion to being a wage slave working for other people, but his solution was to become a self-employed rag and bone man, very much his own man. He saw no need for collectivism.

Billy and Alice

Billy, the son of William Page, a labourer, was born on 13 October 1883 in the slums of Norwich, at Wilson's Yard in St Martins Oak ward. When he was very young, Wilf visited his grandparents at this yard and remembered his grandmother reading teacups. He also remembered that his own father was very thin because of the bad diet of his slum childhood. Wilf's daughter Carol described Billy as 'an interesting character who survived on his wits'. She remembers him in his cloth cap, smoking Woodbines and listening to the football results. Wilf's mother Alice Randall was 'a strong woman and a powerful role model, with lots of fire and creativity, who wrote poetry'. Alice had been born in 1886, the daughter of an agricultural labourer (though not a union member!), who later became a coalman. This was Thomas Randall, Wilf's maternal grandfather, who would later share his bed – after he had been sacked and made homeless.

Billy Page had started off his activities with a hand-pulled cart, collecting rags and bones in Norwich. As he built up the business he progressed to a horse-drawn cart, and expanded into scrap metal and second-hand furniture. And it was while he was collecting from the house where she was a servant that Billy met Alice.

Alice was from a strong Methodist family and when she introduced Billy to her parents in Wymondham they did not immediately hit it off. On hearing that Alice's father worked five and a half days a week humping sacks of coal for a merchant, on meagre wages, Billy was not impressed. The story was handed down that he told Alice's father:

> I work for myself and what I earn is mine to keep. Humping coal for somebody who keeps most of the profit and gives me a wage I could hardly live on is not my idea of life.

To which his prospective father-in-law replied:

> You should remember what the Bible says, young man. We all have our appointed stations in life. There are men who have to work for others, and others that pay them for that work. If you cannot accept this, you are arguing against the most honest book that was ever written.

Billy could not accept this, and he asked Thomas if he really was happy in his work. When there was no reply Billy exclaimed:

You're not! You're only happy when you can get out into that garden. There you can dig your potatoes, plant your cabbages and carrots, all in your own time. You can make all your own decisions without having to ask anyone else. That's what matters to me. I may not earn the same every week as you do, but at least I'm working for myself and not lining someone else's pockets.

There was an awkward silence until Thomas changed the subject. His loyalty to his employer was to prove misplaced, however, when some time later, as we shall see, he was sacked without notice, to make way for a younger man.

On their way home from this visit Alice rebuked Billy for being too sharp with her parents, and for being 'a brash young man who apparently would earn a pound one day and no more than tuppence the rest of the week'. How would that provide security for a marriage, she asked. Billy became less brash, however, and they were married at the Methodist Wesleyan Chapel in Wymondham on 1 November 1912. Alice's father described himself as an agricultural labourer, rather than a coalman, on the marriage certificate. The wedding was the first time that Alice had met Billy's parents, however, because Billy did not wish her to see the slum conditions in which they lived.

Because of the agricultural recession, Billy found that rusting farm implements in the countryside provided him with a more plentiful supply of scrap iron, and so he concentrated his collection on nearby villages instead of Norwich. To make collecting the scrap easier he and Alice moved to the hamlet of Newton St Faith, which was four or five miles north of Norwich. He now had to push his loaded cart all the way to Norwich, however, in order to sell what he had collected. It was at this time therefore that Billy bought a pony and cart, renting a paddock for the pony near his home, Oak Cottages in the Catton Road.

This was where Wilf was born, on 11 September 1913. The baptism was announced in the *Wymondham & District Free Church Magazine*, and the ceremony was conducted in the local Wesleyan Church by Reverend J. Watson of nearby Attleborough. The baby was baptised as Wilfred Randall Page: Wilfred was a combination of his father's two names – William and Frederick – and Randall was his mother's maiden name. (Interestingly, in the same issue of the magazine that announced the baptism there was an advert for S. Gooch & Sons, blacksmiths; this was the family of Edwin Gooch, who would later become the agricultural union president and a Labour MP, and for whom Wilf would go on to work as agent.) Wilf soon had two new sisters – Vera Maude, born 6 June 1915, and Doreen Amelia, born on 5 September 1916.

On one occasion, when Wilf was three years old, his mother became distraught when he went missing. Eventually she found him in the stable, however, lying against the neck of Tommy, their pony. She admonished him severely and warned him that Tommy could have accidentally trodden on him. But Wilf had formed a strong bond with Tommy, and assured her the pony would never harm him. 'To me Tommy was friend, confidante and source of the greatest pleasure a small boy could have,' he later recalled:

> On summer evenings he would be let into the paddock where I got him used to standing by a fallen tree. The tree was ideally placed for me to climb on to and mount him. He would wait patiently until I was securely seated before breaking into a trot, and sometimes a gallop, around the fenced paddock. It

was the highlight of the day, and one of the happiest of my boyhood memories.

The outbreak of war in 1914 had strongly boosted Billy's business, since the government was increasingly in need of scrap metal for arms production, and this had greatly increased its price. In addition, farm workers were now in full employment again, producing food for the nation at war; and they were also getting paid for overtime – so they had more money to spend on items such as second-hand furniture. Both sides of Billy's business were therefore prospering. In fact he had more work than he could handle, and Alice now took over the furniture side.

This prosperity was short-lived, however. Billy was conscripted into the army (the Queen's Royals, West Surrey regiment), and Alice soon discovered that the allowances granted to army wives were pitifully small. And circumstances did not improve when Billy was discharged from the army in 1918 after a series of illnesses. As soon as the war ended the demand for scrap metal dropped dramatically, and farm workers lost their overtime – and with it their ability to buy second-hand furniture.

School and chapel

In 1919, when Wilf was six, things were made worse for him when he was forced to attend school – which he hated – in Horsham St Faith, a mile and a half away. On the first day of school his mother gave him a bright red jersey and cap to wear, and took him there in the pony and cart. 'I discovered how cruel children can be to somebody they see as different from themselves,' he remembered. 'Arriving in a horse and cart was bad enough. Then they picked on the red jersey and shouted Tomato! Tomato!, and that caught on as my name.' He told his mother he would never wear the jersey again, and, like the others, would walk to school and back.

Walking to school, however, meant he was easily distracted by the pleasures of the countryside. 'I would search the rushes for moorhens' nests with their speckled brown eggs, and gather wild flowers,' he reminisced. 'After this pleasant detour I often did not reach school until the other children were having their mid morning break.'

Expecting to be punished, he gave the flowers he had picked to his teacher, Miss Nunn, and told her all about the birds and wildlife he had seen. She smiled and marked the register as though he had arrived on time. His late arrivals began to get more frequent, however, partly because his duties included tending to the family's pigs, goat and ducks on the way to school. On sunny days he found it difficult to tear himself away from the pond where he took the ducks.

The disciplinarian headmaster, Mr Harry Leadbetter, was not as forgiving as Miss Nunn, and Wilf would often be caned on the hands and backside. On some occasions the boys used to take the canes and hide them in the back of the piano during break times. 'After a while the old piano didn't work so they had to get the piano tuner in to have a look, and all these canes rolled out,' recalled Wilf.

Wilf even came into confrontation with the headmaster for being too good at poetry. The headmaster had asked all the pupils to write a poem at the weekend, to show to him on the following Monday. Wilf had already developed a love of writing essays and poetry, and therefore set about the task with relish. On the designated day he submitted his work, entitled 'An Ode to a Ship'. But instead of being impressed by the poem, the headmaster accused Wilf of having copied it and ordered him to his office. 'Without any preliminaries he grabbed my tie and dragged me towards him', recalled Wilf. 'Then he quickly turned his chair round as he did when caning boys. I pleaded with him not to beat me, as I was innocent of any wrong.' But Mr Leadbetter accused him of lying, partly on the grounds that he

didn't believe that Wilf would know what an ode was. 'It's a sad poem', Wilf shouted back. 'There's an ode to an umbrella in my Christmas book, and my mother told me what it was.'

Near the school stood St Faith's Union Workhouse, built in 1805 and enlarged in 1853 to accommodate up to 330 inmates (complete with its own 'inspector of nuisances'). The children were told not to walk on the workhouse side of the road, it being alleged that all the people inside had diseases. But on one of the occasions when Wilf was late for school, he dared to walk on that side of the road: 'There was a big high hedge and at the bottom of the hedge there were little holes. As I walked very close this hand came through the hedge and I went to touch and hold it. It was an old lady and she was so pleased she'd got somebody who was touching her who was outside.'

Wilf's mother made him attend Sunday school at the Newton St Faith Primitive Methodist Chapel, which had been built in 1872. At the chapel Wilf soon came across people involved in the trade union movement. Farm union leader George Edwards addressed the chapel once a year, and local preacher Billy Furness, who had joined the agricultural union when it was formed in 1906, spoke there every week. Wilf found Furness fascinating. For Billy Furness the 'good book' was a blueprint for living, and the rules of the union incorporated the Bible's teachings. He hated injustice and was always pointing out instances of the exploitation of workers by their employers.

Wilf recalled him as saying:

When you next go with your father on his rounds to one of those big country houses he calls on, take a look through the windows while he's busy. You'll see how well those people live. Take a look at all the good furniture, the pictures on the wall, the silver on the dining table. Everything you see is made by working people who are probably living in squalor themselves because their wages are so low.

As Wilf commented: 'It was soon apparent to me that Methodist teachings and trade unionism went hand in hand, whereas the Church of England or High Church were associated with the squires, farmers and moneyed people generally':

To illustrate the point Billy Furness persuaded me to attend a service at St Faith's church. I went down the aisle to the front pews and sat down. Before I could settle I was quietly hoisted up and my attention directed to a card reserving the seat for a Mr Spurrel. I had no idea that you could book seats in church. But when I reported back my experience to Billy Furness he explained that Mr Spurrel, the local magistrate, had rented that seat for a year.

The practice was common among the better off. Along with the collections it was their way of keeping the church going. Methodist chapels with their much poorer congregations existed on the pennies and tuppences that were all working people could afford. It was the class system again. There was no equality, even in the House of God.

Family difficulties

A family crisis occurred in 1919, when Thomas Randall, Wilf's grandfather, turned up on their doorstep, homeless: 'The coal merchant had called him in to tell him he had become too old at 62 for delivering their sacks of coal. It was a job for a younger, stronger man. There was no argument, no pension, nothing. Just the sack.' Grandfather Randall's son – Wilf's uncle Walter – was sharing his cottage with him at the time, and had recently married. He now told the old man he would have to move out to make room for his wife. Wilf's mother was aghast at the thought of her own father going into the workhouse, but she was also anxious about adding another inmate to their already overcrowded home. At that time the Pages had two bedrooms and three children. As she told him: 'Unless Billy can think of something when he comes in there's only the outbuildings left'.

On his return Wilf's father was not slow to point out the problems of yet another call on his already stretched resources. 'I can see them now', recalled Wilf. 'My mother, tall and commanding in manner, father smaller and more tense and harassed than usual, and grandfather looking prematurely aged and shrunken.' But they came up with a solution. Wilf and his sister Doreen had until now shared one of the bedrooms, each having a single bed. But Billy remembered that he had an old double bed stored away, so out came Wilf's single bed and in came the double bed, which Wilf and his grandfather now shared. Poor Vera had to sleep on one of the single beds in the corridor.

In January 1920 Vera died at just four years old, having contracted diphtheria. As Wilf recalled:

> The only treatment was a boiling kettle with a very long spout that poured steam into the bedroom, where she fought for breath long and agonisingly. Then, after weeks of taking turns to refill the kettle to maintain the humidity, we saw a change for the worse. A kind neighbour with a fine horse and rubber-tyred gig offered to help. Mother wrapped Vera close to her body and set off for Norfolk and Norwich hospital. On the journey little Vera's strength ebbed away, and she was found to be dead on arrival.

When another daughter was born the following year, on 2 July 1921, she was also named Vera in memory of her sister (though her second name was Alice rather than Maude).

The year 1923 was another difficult year, and it was one of turmoil for Wilf: his father's business was not making enough money for the family to live on, there was a strike against pay cuts by the farmworkers' union, and he organised his own strike at school, for which he was severely punished:

> I had always been close to my father but now when we did the rounds together on the horse and cart he seemed increasingly worried. Instead of the forward-looking optimism that I remembered, nothing made him enthusiastic after his return from the Great War.
>
> He talked more and more of the good old days when he could sell all the scrap metal he could handle, and make

himself money counted in pounds rather than shillings. Look at me now, he would say, messing about with bloody old rabbit and mole skins, a few jars and bottles, worn out bits of clothes that'll only fetch a few pence. What with me and Alice and you kids to feed, I don't know what we'd do without the bits of furniture I pick up.

One day in 1923 Wilf noted that the local menfolk were gathered everywhere, talking in groups or sitting on walls, and – even more surprising to him – there was a presence of uniformed policeman. This was the strike of agricultural workers against wage cuts and increased working hours led by George Edwards (see p26-7). Wilf, who had not yet reached his tenth birthday, was alarmed at the large number of police, who had been brought in from other counties to attack the strikers and protect scabs. He asked his Sunday school teacher Billy Furness for an explanation of the strike. As Wilf later told the story, Billy reached for his Bible and quoted from the Book of Deuteronomy – 'Thou shalt not muzzle the ox that treads the corn':

If the ox was not muzzled it would stop to eat as it went along, so it wouldn't do as much work. At the end of the day the farmer feeds the ox what he thinks is just enough to keep it fit to work the next day.

You can think of the farm worker as a kind of ox, with a muzzle too. His muzzle is the wage his employer decides is just sufficient to keep him in enough food to work and bring up his family. His family would then continue his work when he is too old and weak to do it himself any longer.

What is happening today in this village and others is that because the human ox is more intelligent than the animal, he has formed a union with others like himself. The union has told the employers that the men will not thresh more corn until they receive a larger ration – in other words an increase in wages.

The Horsham school strike

The struggle of the farmworkers inspired Wilf to call his own strike at school in the same year, to try to prevent the leaving of his much loved teacher, Miss Nunn, who was getting married. The children were upset by losing their teacher, but it was the ruling of the education authority that married women could not continue as teachers.

Wilf remembered Miss Nunn as the only teacher in the school who treated the children as human beings. They could not accept that she was to be prevented from teaching them without putting up a fight:

I rallied support among my schoolmates. Councils of war were held in huddled playground groups, and a course of action was decided. On the first day of the strike we assembled at our meeting place and made banners out of sticks and handkerchiefs. Then we marched up and down the road outside the school, shouting our slogans and waving the makeshift banners.

Old Leadbetter stood at the school gates urging us to get back to school, but we were full of enthusiasm for our cause. After an hour or so we felt we'd made our point and retired in good order to our headquarters in the horse pasture. Later we reassembled and marched on the school once more, to the same angry response from the headmaster.

The following morning we marched again, still full of hope that justice would prevail and our favourite teacher would be reinstated. The headmaster's response seemed to indicate a willingness to compromise. 'Come back to school and we'll discuss your grievances', he told us. 'We want our teacher back', somebody shouted. 'Return to school first, then we'll see', was the answer.

The striking pupils said they would think about what the headmaster had said, and returned to the horse pasture. They were under pressure from their parents to end the strike but they did not want to be seen to give in too easily. They therefore returned to tell the headmaster that they would return on Monday (it was by then Thursday afternoon). Mr Leadbetter scowled at them, and told them that it would be better if they returned to their classes then and there.

On the Monday morning we were confronted by a show of strength. Local magistrate Spurrell, the squire, a policeman, and Leadbetter himself waited grimly to dispense their justice. The headmaster picked out six of us who were considered to be the ringleaders and I was one of them. We were summoned one by one to the headmaster's office, while those waiting their turn were further demoralised by the sound of the cane falling on outstretched hands and the cries of pain that accompanied it. We got two vicious canes on both hands. Somehow we felt that he was intending to destroy the revolutionary idea that was in the school – he was more vicious with us on this occasion than he had been when he'd caned us before.

My turn came, and maybe his personal disapproval of me gave extra strength to his arm, for it was the worst of the many canings I had received. Somehow I fought back the tears and returned to the class. There was some comfort for hands that felt on fire being pressed against the ice cold metal frames on the forms we sat on. Gradually through the morning the pain eased.

Of course our teacher was not reinstated, nor were our bruised hands the end of the punishment. We were all put down a class – which meant little enough to me with my meagre scholastic expectations – but it devastated some boys who would otherwise have been able to sit for a scholarship to the Redcap School in Norwich the following year. I am sure they would have passed through that scholarship and gone on to the grammar school. It completely changed and upset the whole way of life for them. This was a grave injustice indeed.

Another death in the family

Another sister for Wilf was born on 25 May 1924, Sylvia Evelyn. This meant another mouth to feed, at a time when their father's business was bringing in less and less money. So the Page family were looking forward to Grandfather Randall reaching his seventieth birthday and qualifying for his old age pension of ten shillings a week. This would bolster their uncertain income. (The Old Age Pension Acts were introduced in 1908, after methodists, trade unionists and others had campaigned for them, and the first old age pensions were paid in 1909.)

With just a month to go, on 31 March 1926, Grandfather Randall died of sclerosis and heart failure in the bed he shared with Wilf – who had gone to school thinking his grandfather was still asleep: 'He had simply died in his sleep and I had known nothing of it. I could not forget that at the moment his spirit had left his body I must have been right next to him, and yet I had been given no sign whatsoever.'

The sum of £25 was now due on a life insurance policy, but the family's finances were so bad that Billy decided not to waste any of it on an undertaker. They carried the old man's coffin to the cemetery two miles away on their own pony and cart. Wilf and his father set off in the early hours of a very cold morning, to avoid being seen transporting the coffin in this unorthodox fashion, and arrived at the cemetery at about 5 am. The parson was not due until 11 o'clock, so they decided to free Tommy the pony from the cart to enjoy the long grass. The horse moved too quickly for them, however, and the cart tipped up in the air. 'The coffin slid off and stood upright with grandfather on his head, and dad used language seldom heard in a cemetery', remembered Wilf. Luckily they managed to get everything back in place before the parson arrived sharp at 11 o'clock:

> When he saw a ponycart in the cemetery his face became distorted with anger. I started leading the pony to the graveside and could hear father telling the parson that grandfather's last wish was for his favourite pony Tommy to take him to his grave. All the parson kept repeating was that this was very unusual.

They now realised that they had forgotten to bring a rope to lower the coffin into the grave. It could not be dropped in without ropes because the wood it was made of was so cheap that it would have burst open on impact. They therefore made the decision to use Tommy's reins. 'This did the trick, and we lowered the coffin slowly into the grave, only to find another problem. Dad could not pull the reins from under the coffin as the buckles were wedged between the ground and the coffin.' As they now realised, too late, they should have placed two pieces of wood in the grave before lowering the coffin, in order to leave a space underneath so that the ropes could be pulled out.

I therefore had to climb into the grave with dad holding the reins. I was able to ease one end of the coffin up and he then pulled the reins out. Then I had to move to the other end of the coffin to repeat the process, after which dad handed me one end of the reins and pulled me out. When I looked up to see the parson standing five or six yards from the grave I was surprised at the fury on his face. He had not offered us any assistance and then gave the shortest burial service ever. We returned home with Tommy at a slow trot and I kept thinking of the stories grandfather used to tell me about the hard times he had had when he was a young man. During the time he had lived with us we had grown very close and I was glad I had been with him at the end.

His father brought him down to earth, remarking: 'We've done a good job today, Wilf, and Tommy had a gutful of lush grass.'

3. Drifting in London and Jersey

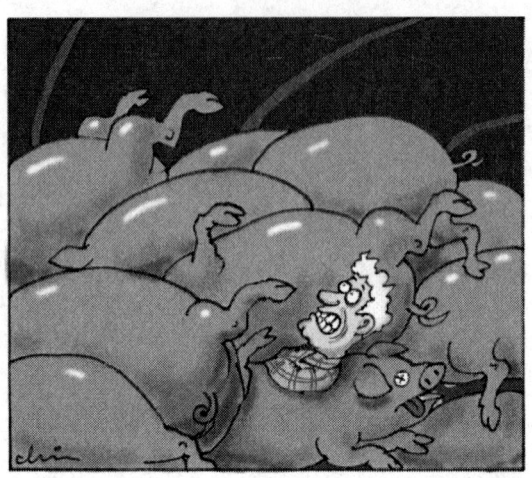

Wilf's school education was cut short when he was just thirteen years old, because he was needed to supplement the family income following an accident to his father. Both his father's legs had been broken, and his jaw smashed by a startled horse, when he had drunkenly fallen from his cart, landing between the shafts and the horse. Wilf had to leave school immediately to help his mother in collecting scrap.

Billy's business had gone from bad to worse, and he had therefore turned to buying and selling horses – a trade which was carried out extensively in pubs. This meant that any profits were usually drunk away, and he tended to come home feeling the worse for wear. Alice had threatened to leave him unless he mended his ways, and Wilf's close relationship with his father had also rapidly deteriorated.

Mother and son earned very little from their efforts and they were beginning to worry that they would starve. Then Alice discovered that a shop and house were available for a low rent in Wymondham. It looked like a heaven-sent opportunity to make a fresh start. Billy was now given an ultimatum – to go with Alice to Wymondham or be left behind when she took the family there on her own. He agreed to go, and the whole family moved to the shop, at Brunswick House in Bridewell Street, Wymondham. Billy earned some money peddling small items of clothing from door to door on his cycle, while Alice sold sweets and other cheap goods in the shop. Wilf – reluctantly – took a job in a furniture factory in Norwich, and had to cycle to and from work, a distance of about nine miles each way. 'For me it was a very different way of life that had no appeal', he said. 'Earning money was marvellous at first, but the novelty wore off very quickly. I was really an outdoor person, and being cooped up all day in a noisy factory under constant supervision came hard.'

For a while Wilf joined his father on his round, but he hated anything to do with selling and was no good at it, and the pair were always quarrelling. Then his mother found an advert for a vacancy as kitchen boy for a Major and Lady Bosanquet at Weston Park in Hertfordshire. 'It wouldn't have been my choice, but I knew I had to get away from the awful atmosphere at home,' said Wilf.

A uniformed chauffeur was waiting to pick Wilf up when he got off the coach at Baldock. The chauffeur shouted 'Mr Page! Is there a Mr Page there?'. This was the first time that Wilf had been addressed in this way – rather than as plain Wilf – and it took him a while to realise he was being hailed. In just a few months he had changed from a schoolboy into a grown-up 'mister'. Any delusions of grandeur were rapidly dispelled, however, when they arrived at the house and he was inspected like a horse by her ladyship. 'He looks fairly healthy, though a bit thin perhaps,' she observed to the cook. 'But we can feed him and get him going. I think he'll make an ideal lad for you in the kitchen.' This reminded Wilf of the times when his father had showed his mother a new horse, pointing out its finer points.

Wilf now had to be up at 5.30 every morning to light the stove to make it hot enough for cooking by 6.30. But after he had on a number of occasions failed to ignite the coal, and made a mess of his other duties – such as cleaning the pans, washing the vegetables and scrubbing the kitchen floor – the cook became enraged, frequently reporting him to their employer. Instead of being sacked, however, he was transferred to the pantry, where he worked for the butler, 'serving meals in blue trousers, white shirt with dicky-bow, and a smart black and white striped short coat. White gloves completed the uniform, and the work was much cleaner and more agreeable':

But my first attempt at serving came close to disaster. Balancing a sauce boat and spoon on a silver salver, I went to serve the Major when I felt the tray tip slightly. It was just enough to unbalance the long spoon, which came out of the sauce boat, hit the edge of the tray and fell to the floor. I dared not bend down to get the spoon for fear of upsetting the soup all over the Major, so without really thinking I blurted out to the Major: 'I'm sorry, could you pick it up?'.

The Major's eyes met mine, first with a shocked expression and then with a twinkle. There was absolute silence for a moment before the butler rushed across, apologising profusely, and picked up the spoon. The others seemed to be enjoying a private joke while I wished the floor would open up and swallow me.

A few days later, on his day off, Wilf came across a football match on the village green and stopped to watch it. When the ball came to him on the touch line he automatically hoofed the ball, which hit the goal crossbar. The players rushed over to tell him what a good shot it had been from such a distance, and to invite him to join the team. Wilf joined up and became a regular in the team, which competed in a league, but was finally dropped when Major Bosanquet refused to give him time off to travel to an away fixture, which would have involved a long journey by coach: he had to be available to serve Saturday lunch at 1 pm. The captain of the team reluctantly explained that he needed players who could be called on for every match.

After a couple of years at Weston Park, Wilf, by now aged 16, was getting restless. He felt that waiting at table was not a job for a man to be doing. He left and became an upholstery apprentice for a short while, but that did not suit him either. He returned to Wymondham, but within a week was heading for London with his friend Bob Cracke, whose parents ran the pub next door to Wilf's mother's shop.

A driver who every day took dead pigs from the nearby village of Besthorpe to Smithfield Market in London gave them a lift:

> Because of Bob's asthma it was decided that he should travel in the front of the lorry with the driver and I had to travel in the back, lying on top of the pigs that had been slaughtered and cleaned up that day. The pigs were icy cold and there was just enough room to move when the tarpaulin was pulled over the load. I was in complete darkness. The lorry seemed to find every bump in the road, and I lost all sense of time. The swaying of the chassis dislodged one of the pig carcasses, which fell on top of me. I called out that I was trapped, but my

voice could not be heard over the din of the engine. So there I was, trapped beneath the weight of a large dead pig, forced against the cold bodies of those beneath, and shivering as the cold seeped into me.

I passed out at some stage and when the tarpaulin was raised at Smithfield at six o'clock in the morning I was found motionless beneath the pig. Helping hands pulled it off and lifted me out of the lorry and into a nearby cafe where efforts were made to revive me. I remember gradually thawing out with my hands around a big mug of hot tea, welcoming the feeling of warmth spreading slowly through me. It had been a close thing. A few more miles down the road and I might not have survived.

The boys had no work and very little money. Wilf had a national insurance card from his work as a servant, and so was able to claim dole (unemployment benefit) of twelve shillings and sixpence a week, and that kept them going:

We had to buy just cheap food, but we couldn't get anywhere to stay so we were sleeping rough in Green Park. The *News of the World* was a very big paper [this was before it turned tabloid] and it used to cover us up very well in those days. We used to wrap ourselves in that on the seats. But being out at night in London was terrible because it was quite unnatural and lonely. The longer you stayed there the more dishevelled you got. We used to go into the men's toilets at Charing Cross to try and look a bit respectable, get a bit of a wash. We both felt somehow we shouldn't have left home and then we felt if we did go back we'd be a failure. We'd got to stay as we'd burned our boats and told all our mates that we were going up to London to earn some money.

The two youngsters decided to go their separate ways, Bob to work in a Brixton pub, which his father had arranged, and Wilf to stay in Plaistow in the east end, with the Savage family, with whom his father had been billeted during the war more than ten years earlier. The families had not been in touch since the war, however, so Wilf was surprised at the warm welcome he received: the Savages remembered his father well. They could only put Wilf up for a few days, however. They could not risk a longer stay for fear of being accused of taking in lodgers and having their unemployment benefit stopped. But they put the word out among their friends and, with a display of true east end hospitality, each put him up for a few days in turn, until he got a bartender's job, living in at Ladbroke Grove.

Although Wilf was totally inexperienced in bar work the head barman who interviewed him was impressed by his frank and honest confession: 'I don't know anything about bar work, but I'm very quick at picking things up.' Between them they worked out a ruse to conceal his inexperience from the landlord – an alcoholic who did not surface until noon, at which time he picked up his daily bottle of whisky before retiring again. They made sure Wilf was working in the cellar during this brief interlude. After a week or so Wilf was proficient at the job and no longer needed to engage in this hide and seek. But the job was not to last. The boss's liver gave out after a while and he died after a violent attack of delirium tremens. The new owners made a clean sweep of existing staff, leaving Wilf again looking for a job and lodgings.

He found both in another pub, the Hop Poles, in Hammersmith. 'At first it was good to be working and have a few shillings to spend,' he said. 'But the staff had a way of life that didn't suit me. Their leisure time seemed to be spent drinking after hours, then taking whisky from the bar to the nearby flat of some obliging floosies, and getting up to all sorts of sexual shenanigans that they'd boast about, bleary eyed, next day.' Wilf reluctantly gave in to peer pressure to join his workmates in these crude activities, but guilt from his strict upbringing stopped him from enjoying it. This lifestyle continued much the same as he drifted in and out of other pub work, and after a while he decided it was time for another change. His friend Bob Cracke felt the same, so together they embarked on the ferry to Jersey in the Channel Islands, hoping to qualify as chefs in one of the hotels, and then get well paid jobs in Paris or London. 'There was no money in our budget for hotels, but luckily we came across a derelict porter's hut on the railway station of a small village where the line had been closed down. It was empty and uninviting, but there was a bench on which we slept as best we could.'

They discovered that it was too early in the season for hotel work, and that picking potatoes was just about the only casual work they were likely to find. This work, on a local farm, was to prove much more back-breaking than they had anticipated. 'The fields were steep and the first thing we found was that there was no equipment, so everything had to be done by hand,' recalled Wilf:

We were assigned to work with a wiry old Breton, who certainly knew what he was doing. Without apparently hurrying himself, he expertly forked the rows, sending the potato heads one way and the crop the other. We had to pick up all the potatoes we could find, brush off excess dirt, and put them into a hand-held skip. It sounded easy until we found that we had to work flat out, occasionally stopping to rest aching backs, while the tireless old Breton drew further away from us. By lunch time he was rows and rows ahead. Nor did it help to watch the others – Bretons working in pairs were forking and picking up in unison. How the hell did they do it, we asked ourselves a hundred times. At three o'clock in the afternoon the farmer, sympathetic but firm, insisted we were not suitable for the job. This work will kill you, he warned. Come and see me when we finish work today and I'll pay you off. We found that hard to accept, and when the others stopped for the day, miles ahead of us, we laboured on as best we could until it became too dark to see what we were doing. Perhaps this impressed the farmer, for when we staggered to the farmhouse, hardly able to stand upright for the pain in our legs and back, he paid us 25 shillings each – almost a week's wages for a Norfolk farm labourer at the time.

Earning that much money in one day went to their heads and they set off to explore the delights of St Helier. One of the main attractions was a dance hall, of great interest to Wilf, who had learned to dance at the Hammersmith Palais when working in London. 'In no time at all we were offered the job of dancing with elderly dowagers, who were flattered to have young escorts. For this we were supplied with a decent suit and bow tie. I must have looked quite a sight dressed up like that.' But after a few weeks the glamour wore off and they became bored, and not a little embarrassed at their gigolo status. By then, however, the season was picking up and work was available in the hotels. They got jobs cleaning kitchens in the Merton House Hotel, where the wages were low but the tips generous. This kept them going until the end of the summer when they returned on the ferry back to England.

Back in London, working as a barman again in the Alexandra Hotel, Clapham Common, Wilf found himself slipping back to the bad old ways of going out boozing and womanising after hours. He had a compulsion to join his fellow workmates, gaining a sense of excitement from their roistering, yet he could not escape a sense of guilt from his early chapel upbringing. Going to bed one night after a particularly rowdy session, fuddled with whisky fumes, the realisation dawned on him. If his life was to change he must exercise

some self discipline. Otherwise, he feared, he would end up 'a raddled old soak that nobody will employ'.

It was December 1932. Wilf was on his day off, walking past two Horse Guards in Whitehall, when his thoughts turned to joining the army. So, nuzzling up to one of the motionless horses he asked one of the guards 'how do you get into your lot?' He had to repeat the question several times before the guard replied in a mumble out of the corner of his mouth, without turning his head. The guard told Wilf he would have to do years of square bashing before having a chance to perform a duty such as his. Then, full of bitterness, he added:

Don't have anything to do with this work. It's nothing but spit and polish. Just look at this harness – some bloody kid has given my horse chocolate and it has got all over the bit. There will be hell to pay. See these trousers? We have to blanco them, which takes hours and hours. If there is just a tiny spot missed the sergeant major orders it done all over again. Ugh, it's a horrible bloody job. Don't think of having anything to do with it, son.

Wilf, effectively discouraged, wandered on to the House of Commons and approached the policeman on duty at the entrance. Again he asked 'how do you get into your lot?', adding 'you've got nice warm clothes on, a good pair of boots, you look well fed and get a pension at the end of it. That'd suit me fine.' The policeman gave him a scornful look and replied:

Don't you believe it. You don't get any pension these days. Don't you know there's an economic crisis? Now they get rid of you and get another youngster in … like you in fact. They're not going to give you a pension for nothing. I want to get out of this lot myself in fact. There's a corrugated iron shed opposite the war memorial, over the other side of the square. It's got a sign outside for Royal Air Force vacancies. I'm thinking of joining them.

Wilf decided to explore this possibility himself. And so, after the briefest of medical tests and a few simple sums to solve, he was accepted into the RAF at the age of 19. His RAF record shows he was 5 foot 11 inches tall (two years later he was to grow to 6 foot), had brown hair, blue eyes, a fresh complexion, and a small reddish mark on the left side of his nose. He was told to report for duty in the new year, on 15 January 1933, for a trial period of three days, after which he could leave or be sworn in.

On his last night at home he sat at the hearth with his parents. His mother lectured him 'on the pitfalls of boozing and women with venereal diseases', as he later recalled. 'Dad warned me that I would not get much pay so I should try to get a little extra by playing Crown and Anchor.' This was an illegal gambling game common in the forces, which his father remembered from the first world war. 'Sitting on the hearth rug he drew a Crown and Anchor board, and told me that the secret was to get control of the bank. Then he showed me how to place bets so you could not lose.'

4. The RAF years

'Get off that ruddy lorry, you're like a load of ruptured crabs,' a sergeant screamed at the twelve recruits on their arrival at West Drayton RAF reception centre.

This was followed by three days of abusive and foul language from the sergeant, who made the men get up at dawn to do a series of pointless chores. It was too much for four of the recruits, and they decided to drop out. The remaining eight were sworn in on 18 January 1933 – including Wilf. His number was 516200 – stamped on his cutlery and remembered by him for the rest of his life. After they had been sworn in, there was a complete transformation in the sergeant; he shook their hands and explained that he was under orders to be 'a bastard', to make sure the men truly wanted to stay in the force. Up till that moment they had had a chance to leave, but now they were in for the duration. After about a week the new recruits were transferred to Uxbridge; they had been selected to take part in the Royal Tournament in Olympia. This meant they had six months of doing nothing except physical training, and this suited Wilf down to the ground.

Wilf soon made friends with another of the recruits, a Londoner called Dan Cohen, who was Jewish and a Marxist. When he was walking past the toilets one day Wilf had heard fighting going on inside, and then seen four men holding Dan down and scrubbing him with industrial brushes. They were shouting 'we'll scrub you dirty Jew white'. Wilf got stuck in on Dan's side – 'I was fairly useful with my fists in those days' – and the attackers fled:

> I got him back to his bed, and he was very shaken. I asked him what it was all about. 'Well', he said, 'Mussolini is in power in Italy and it looks as if Hitler is going to get in power in Germany. It is all based on anti-Jewish feeling and there's a spill-off in this country. The whole western world is developing this stuff.'

Dan went into further details and told Wilf that he was a communist:

> He used to talk to me about the frictions within the world, why anti-semitism was an historic problem, and explained the economics of capitalism. He thought the Soviet Union was a new experiment that was going to succeed and produce a new world society. He stirred my imagination for two reasons. One was his approach to the business, and, secondly, he was saying things my old Sunday School teacher used to say about world problems, the wealthy, and the poor. Dan was doing the same thing but at a much higher level.
>
> I got quite attracted to it and he got some pamphlets for me to read. He told me not to let other people see me reading them but to take them into the toilet. It was all very conspiratorial because distributing communist propaganda

in the forces was looked on as virtually a treasonable offence.

But of course the language was too much for me. The expropriation of the expropriated was one term I remember. What the hell was that all about? Imperialism, lumpen proletariat and other words were quite new to me, so I had to get a dictionary. I used to sit in the toilet with a dictionary in one hand and this bloody pamphlet in the other, trying to work out what it was all about. Then I used to come out and Dan would explain it all to me. He was a wonderful teacher, using very elementary language, and we became good friends.

The first classic novel that Wilf ever read was lent to him by Dan – *The Cloister and the Hearth,* by Charles Reade, first published in 1861.

Wilf and Dan went their separate ways after the Royal Tournament but were to be reunited shortly afterwards on an RAF aerial photographers' course at Farnborough. Wilf had found out about the course in August 1933 while working as a message runner at Biggin Hill (after he had read the message announcing the course it had somehow mysteriously failed to be put on the board for others to read). Wilf relished the scientific study and analysis of light on the course: 'It was my first real education'. He enthused about this to Dan, who replied: 'That's a scientific study of light. Now we will do a scientific study of society. You can break society into different colourings as you can light. You get different forces within society which have driven it on from cavemen to feudalism and then to capitalism.' Dan maintained that capitalism was in its final stages and socialism had come about. 'I could begin to see society in depth', said Wilf. 'It was new and exciting to me.'

Wilf passed the course as a photographer and in September

1935 was posted to Upper Heyford near Oxford. It was here that the 22-year-old Wilf met a pretty 15-year-old nurse at a dance. Her name was Christina Beesley. Before long Wilf had become a frequent visitor to her home for tea (according to Christina, he was also attracted to her sister, who was three years older).

After Wilf had introduced Christina to the communist paper, the *Daily Worker*, the discovery that his daughter was buying the paper nearly led to her being thrown out of her home by her father – Thomas Beesley was an arch Tory. He was a carpenter who made coffins, and Christina used to help him by making the linings for them and delivering them. 'A lot of them were never paid for – poor people couldn't afford it', she recalled. 'So they used to pay my father in kind, perhaps sending round a horse and cart-load of manure for the garden.'

Four years later, in 1939, Wilf and Christina were to marry, but at the end of 1935 they had to part when Wilf was posted to India. He left from Southampton on the troopship Somersetshire with a mixture of RAF and army soldiers.

The trip to India

On the long four-week sea voyage Wilf and all the non-officers were crammed into the uncomfortably hot lower deck, while the much more comfortable upper deck was reserved for the officers and their wives. There was also a difference in the toilets between officers and other ranks. The officers had separate and private toilets, but the men had to sit on toilet seats in a communal line on deck: 'I remember one of my colleagues vomiting into a toilet at the front end of the ship and his false teeth came out and went down the pan. He had to rush to the back end of the row of toilets to catch them before they were thrown into the sea.'

Wilf volunteered to box for his unit, because it allowed him to exercise on the top deck in the fresh air every day. This was a further sharp lesson in class differences. He saw officers and their ladies lounging on the deck in their deckchairs, sipping cool drinks, while the men were sweating below decks. And he was also to learn another lesson, during a boxing bout. He took part in a fight in the well of the ship, while the officers and ladies looked down on them from the rails (which made Wilf think he was just there to amuse them). However his attention was distracted from this thought – and the boxing – when he spotted among the onlookers a young woman who was smiling invitingly at him, her breasts clearly visible under her light cotton dress. The distraction proved fatal: Wilf's opponent delivered a punch which sent him onto the canvass and defeat.

While still on the ship the men were treated to some advice from an officer, which reflected the institutional racism in the colonial forces at that time. They were warned about the 'cunning and devious wiles of the natives, whether brown, black or yellow – they're all heathen oriental devils'. Further advice was to give no money to beggars, and to 'ignore women who only want to lure you to some dark corner, relieve you of your money, and give you the clap in return for a moment's not so cheap thrill'. Finally they were advised not to have anything to do with the Indians, who were described as 'a filthy, lazy lot of devils, not to be trusted'.

On disembarking in Karachi they marched to the railway station for a four-day train journey to the interior. Wilf was shocked by the plight of the beggars he saw on the way, especially the children squatting in the dust, with flies settling on their faces that they only half heartedly tried to brush away. Wherever he went he was made painfully aware of the terrible poverty of the majority of Indians. He felt he had to let people know about it back home, so he wrote a letter to the parson in Wymondham, indignantly detailing in vivid terms the misery endured by the common people in the richest country in the British Empire. The parson calmly advised patience: 'the rulers of our great empire are already doing much to raise the well being of the natives'. Wilf wrote back angrily, rejecting this complacency, and arguing that 'the English people are just making money here and there is no attempt to uplift the Indians at all'. He received no further reply. And his sense of outrage at the British attitude to the Indians was further increased when he was in Lahore. There he saw a notice that proclaimed: 'The shooting of Indians from the balconies shall cease forthwith'. The fact that the notice dated from before the first world war did not alleviate his distaste.

During this period Wilf continued his boxing career as a middleweight. One of his opponents was an Indian boxer known as 'the Karachi Sailor'. 'He was good and we often did exhibition bouts together,' said Wilf. Wilf also played cricket for a team of airmen against a team of Indians – but they had to drink separately afterwards.

After about a year in India Wilf was selected for further training as an aerial photographer, and was moved to Ambala, eighty miles north of Delhi. This was an expanding field of work for the RAF in India, which was co-operating with the army in controlling the North West frontier, along the Afghanistan border. The photographs were used to map out the region to assist the army on the ground. The soldiers used the maps to avoid marching through hills, where they were easy targets for the tribesmen – who were suspected of being backed by the

Soviet Union from its nearby border. The technology was quite rudimentary: photographs were taken through a hole in the floor of the small aircraft. This demanded a high degree of skill in the co-ordination of hand and eye, to judge the right moment to click the camera shutter. Wilf showed a natural flair for the art and became one of its leading practitioners, and he was also given the task of training others. He was in his element flying around Mount Everest and other mountains:

> Up at five o'clock in the morning we would see ten different peaks, all different colours, when the sun was rising. We used to have fun sometimes going up as high as the engine would take us before it ran out of oxygen and the plane would start slipping back.

An earthquake in Ambala in 1936 made many Indians homeless, reducing them to begging. Wilf recalled: 'Sadly our boys only gave the girls money after taking them into the showers for sex'. There were two brothels in Ambala but their licences were bought by religious organisations and closed down. Wilf was in a group of five airmen who were taken – as an alternative – to visit some Indian female students in the country. While four went with their partners among the trees, Wilf sat with 'a shy lovely Indian lass who could not speak English': 'I gave her the money, about ten rupees, and held her hand looking at her beautiful eyes. She waited for me to pounce, smiling in a coy way. Such a young kid, I thought, not knowing what she is letting herself in for. So nothing happened.' He also witnessed a plague of locusts in Ambala: 'They were everywhere, like a blanket, eating up vegetation as it went along.'

A training manual that spelled out the dangers of flying in India was kept by Wilf all his life. It included the warning that the hotter air and the different atmosphere meant that planes had less lift than pilots were accustomed to in England. 'That sinking feeling,' it said, 'is a fruitful source of accidents to newcomers.' Another piece of advice was to shake out flying clothing and helmets before putting them on, since 'scorpions have a great fancy for curling up inside for a quiet snooze and hate being disturbed'. How to deal with a large vulture that crashes into you, however, was not covered in the manual. Yet this freak circumstance once confronted Wilf when he was photographing the mountains in a small bi-plane on the Brazerian Front, near the Afghan border. He heard a sound like an explosion, after which the plane started spinning out of control. The pilot pointed to the wing and there Wilf saw a huge vulture that had collided with the plane and become stuck in the struts between the upper and lower wings. Its considerable weight on one side was making the light craft unstable, and it was dropping down towards the valley below. Wilf was given the unenviable task of crawling out on to the wing, 2000 feet above the mountains, and releasing the vulture – not sure whether it was dead or not: 'I was relieved to be alive after that'.

Intimations of resistance

Back on the ground he was only dimly aware of the growing nationalist movement that was uniting Hindus and Muslims to campaign for Indian independence from British rule. But one memorable incident brought home to him its strength, when Pandit Nehru came to Ambala to address a mass rally organised by the Congress Party. Nehru flew into the RAF base, where a car was waiting to take him into the town, and as he alighted from his plane the officer in charge of the base barred his way, demanding the payment of a landing fee. Nehru responded very sharply that, as a matter of principle, he had no intention of paying to land on his own native soil. There followed a tense stand-off for several minutes before the officer backed down, realising there might be a riot as a huge number of Indians streamed by. This prompted much discussion by Wilf and others in the barrack room afterwards.

Wilf knew, from discussions with the Indian pilots he had trained, that they were in sympathy with Gandhi's aims and tactics. He relayed these conversations back to his mates in the billet, where there was general agreement that the policy of putting Congress leaders in jail only led to their cause gaining even more popular support.

At this time Wilf also went with an Indian acquaintance on a bicycle trip into the countryside, to see village life. His most memorable sight there was of an Indian doctor conducting a clinic in an old wooden hut, lit only by a torch strapped to his forehead. Using only rudimentary instruments he was removing cataracts from his patients' eyes. There were over twenty people desperately queuing for this much needed treatment, without which they could lose their livelihoods. Wilf felt a pang of guilt, comparing this to the treatment he had received in a clean, well-equipped military hospital.

Wilf's treatment had been for a severe bout of both malaria and dysentery, and he had been in hospital for over a month:

I remember feeling a sting on the back of my hand from a mosquito and then collapsing on the way for a beer in the canteen. I then got dysentery in the hospital, maybe from the food. The diet was poor at the time. Often we just had dumplings with holes in them and were told if we did not like them we could fuck them.

His comrades in the rugby and football teams were so convinced that he was going to die that they practised firing the military salute over his prospective grave.

Wilf's life had also been endangered on a previous occasion, when he had been left stranded by his colleagues in a rocky semi-desert region. He had been seconded to an artillery unit, and had spent two days in gruelling work, setting up ground to air communication systems. After this he had slept soundly, but when he awoke the next morning he found that the others had departed, leaving him behind with nothing to eat or drink, and without transport. Fortunately he was able to follow the still-fresh wheel tracks left by the gun carriages, but the heat was so intense that he became increasingly concerned for his survival. Then, at a point where two trails merged, he came across a local old man, accompanied by two children, on a cart pulled by a bullock. Through sign language they made it clear they were all going in the same direction and Wilf was allowed to ride on the cart. Eventually they arrived in Hisar, where the guns of the artillery unit were parked under trees, hiding them from spotter planes. Wilf was very angry with the men who had deserted him. He realised only too well that as a uniformed member of a military occupying force he could have been killed if he had run into nationalists who did not subscribe to Gandhi's non-violent approach.

All this made him ponder his own role in the ongoing war against the tribes along the North West frontier. Only recently he had been ordered to assist the army's policy of attacking local forces of resistance. He had been told to shoot at anything that moved in the hills – not with his camera but with a machine gun. He had fired a hundred rounds at the bushes below, hoping nobody was there, and had been glad when this seemed likely since no fire was returned. He was also glad that he was never ordered to drop the bombs he carried.

In 1938 his unit was put on alert to go to Prague and defend Czechoslovakia from invasion by Hitler's Germany. But then Neville Chamberlain's appeasement policy led to a temporary 'peace'. The men knew that war was imminent however – a prospect welcomed by some Indians:

> A lad in my photo-processing department said that Indians welcomed a war where white people would be killing each other and letting India get its freedom. I was then told to ignore him because he was a communist! One of the English pilots, Vivian Van Damm (from the family that ran the Windmill Theatre in London's Soho), discussed it with me and said the Indian could well be right as the empire would disappear because we would not be able to police it.

On one occasion Wilf recalled being shaved by an Indian barber: 'he could hear us talking about black bastards while he had a razor around our throats, so he could easily have taken revenge if he had wanted to'. On another occasion: 'After being fired at in the air at night we suspected it might be some of the Indian troops who were supposed to be protecting us. So we gave them some tracer bullets and sure enough the next time we were fired on we found tracer bullets.' Another time, when out cross-country running Wilf came across some Indians washing laundry in a stream and chanting: 'Black man good, white man bastard':

> I thought if we were in the same position we would do the same, it was like the working class making up rhymes about their bosses at home ... We were always told the Indians were

a sub-standard race, but the officers were always servile to rich Indians on the North West Frontier. We were also told the British were there to keep Muslims, Hindus and Sikhs apart, but we saw them all mixing OK and playing sports together without any problem.

Before long the men were ordered back to Britain to take on the dreaded Nazi Luftwaffe. When their ship docked at Karachi some of them, including Wilf, were detailed to go into the sick bay and pick up three lads with 'Dulally Tap' (a mental illness brought on by the heat):

> Because it was too hot below deck for them they were put inside a rope-ball cage on deck and given sedatives to keep them quiet. I was inside it with one of them one day when the parson came by and thought I was one of them. I was very worried that I might not be released and would never be free again. It was a very traumatic experience.

At Port Said they were allowed off the ship for a swim. Some Egyptian trading boats berthed alongside. 'The ship's kitchen staff threw slops and all kinds of filth over them, which disgusted me,' said Wilf. 'After that the Egyptians shouted out: Mussolini good, English bastards go home!'

Marriage and war

Back home, in August 1939 Wilf was posted to Upper Heyford again, and renewed contact with Christina Beesley. The two were married at St Mary the Virgin church in North Aston, Oxford, on 4 November 1939, just after the outbreak of war.

Wilf encouraged Christina to read socialist books such as

Robert Tressell's *The Ragged Trousered Philanthropists*, Phyllis
Bottome's *The Mortal Storm*, and Jack London's *The Iron Heel*:
'When he came home on leave he wouldn't make love until I
had said what I had read'. Christina went to live with Wilf's
parents in Wymondham, and the cottage became very crowded
again, especially after the young couple's children were born,
Carol in 1941 and John in 1944.

Wilf's war was uneventful on the whole. The nearest to active
service he came was making several flights over the North Sea
searching for signs of German submarines or warships, but
without incident. After a spell instructing new airmen in the
science and mathematics of aerial photography, he was
seconded to the Army Bureau of Current Affairs (ABCA),
which had been formed to boost the morale of the troops and let
them know what they were supposedly fighting for. This gave
Wilf the opportunity to lecture on various developments all over
the world, and on what would happen after the war: 'This
included the prospects of building a new world, and everyone
had utopian ideas'.

The scheme had nearly been dropped however: the military
establishment was deeply suspicious of this aspect of ABCA, as
was the prime minister, Winston Churchill. Churchill thought
that encouraging political discussion in the armed forces would
undermine discipline, and on 8 October 1941 had ordered that
the courses be suspended. But when Secretary of State for War
David Margesson passed on this order to his Permanent Under
Secretary, P.J. Grigg, Grigg consulted General Ron Adam – who
was aghast at the order. Grigg then opened a drawer in his desk,
placed the order at the back, and casually remarked: 'I wonder if
he remembers his notes?' This was very risky for a civil servant,
but his hunch proved correct; it appeared that Churchill had
entirely forgotten the whole matter. The scheme went ahead,

and W.E. Williams (editor of the Workers' Education Association journal *The Highway*) was appointed as its director. In 1942 a similar current affairs discussion scheme was introduced into the RAF.

Wilf took to his new task with gusto, and found he had a natural flair for gauging the mood of his audience and engaging their interest. This prompted some lively discussion, and proved a valuable training ground for Wilf's future public speaking in the cause of the labour movement. There were official guidelines on the contents of the lectures, which could be pretty bland, especially on subjects such as the empire and the future of the colonial peoples. Wilf tended to disregard the guidelines, however, and open such issues up to controversy to ensure a lively response – though he had to be more circumspect when high-ranking officers chose to sit in on the proceedings.

The subject that stimulated most interest and discussion was the shape of post-war Britain; there was a longing for a fairer and more just society. This became a particularly hot issue after the Beveridge Report was published in December 1942. Its author, William Beveridge, outlined a policy to eradicate the 'five evils' of society: poverty, ignorance, squalor, hunger and disease. He advocated social insurance to provide for those in need – or 'care from the cradle to the grave' as it became known. Churchill was furious that a report advocating such sweeping social change had been drafted without his knowledge, and published before he had a chance to veto it. And when a summary of the report was issued in an ABCA bulletin, he ordered the War Office to withdraw it, banning ABCA from organising any discussion of it. But the report was being publicised widely in the press and radio, so that there was no feasible way to enforce such a ban. It was certainly discussed with great interest by Wilf and his group, who thought the Beveridge proposals were nothing less than a just reward for all the suffering and sacrifices of the war.

In May 1943 Wilf, by now a Sergeant, was recommended for a commission, and, having represented the RAF at both boxing and rugby, had high hopes of being successful. But he was turned down, for reasons not specified on his official RAF record. He had been awarded two good conduct badges, in 1936 and 1941, and been promoted several times – in 1935 from Aircraftsman second class to Aircraftsman first class, in 1936 to Leading Aircraftsman, in 1939 to Corporal, and in 1941 to Technical Sergeant. Wilf was convinced that his further promotion had been blocked because of two incidents that remained on his confidential files from India. In one incident he had defended the job of his Indian servant, who had been told by his head man that he would be replaced (by another Indian who could afford to bung him more for the job). Indignant at this blatant injustice, Wilf had rushed into the Squadron Leader's office and protested so vigorously that the decision was reversed. The second incident also involved challenging corruption in the system. When Wilf was put in charge of the Christmas club, he had decided to ignore the Indian head man who usually supplied drink at an exorbitant price, instead buying it from the local bazaar, where it was much cheaper. This time the Squadron Leader, who was probably in receipt of his own back-hander from the middle man, was furious; he accused Wilf of being a bloody troublemaker.

In both cases Wilf had been standing up against corruption and injustice within the system. But when all this emerged at his promotion interview, it seemed that this kind of conduct had made him unsuitable to become an officer and a gentleman. This official view had no doubt been reinforced when he had started to buy the *Daily Worker*, leaving it in the sergeant's mess for others to read.

In June 1943, after Wilf had been posted to Scotland, he attended a Communist Party rally near where he was stationed, in Dundee. The main speaker was the leader of the French Communist Party, Jacques Duclos, who, together with his fellow communist deputies, had been imprisoned in Algiers by the Vichy government. They had been released only five months earlier. Duclos was in Britain at the invitation of General Charles De Gaulle, to discuss terms for the communists to join the National Committee for the Liberation of France. There was a rapturous welcome for Duclos from members of the Free French Army, who made up a large part of the audience, and were keen to hear news of the fight-back by the resistance movement against their country's occupation. There were also many other allied service men and women present at the rally, and they all gave a resounding endorsement to the call for a second front, to relieve the hard pressed Red Army and hasten the liberation of France. This rousing meeting strengthened Wilf's conviction that the only worthwhile future was a socialist one – and that he was not isolated in this belief.

The second front was eventually mounted by the allies, and the long gruelling war was won at last. Wilf was demobbed in November 1945, finally ending his 13 years in the RAF.

5. Labour Party agent and councillor

Delighted as he was to be demobbed and reunited with his young family, Wilf had difficulty in readjusting to civilian life at first, particularly to the routine of seeking work. 'Somehow or another I just couldn't face going to someone to ask them to employ me,' he explained:

> I'd been in the air force where my wages had come every Friday without my even thinking about it. Then suddenly I was having to ask somebody could they give me a job. I just couldn't do it. I went through a terrible ordeal because my wife and kiddies needed supporting. It was one of the worst periods of my life, wondering what I was going to do.

Living once more in Wymondham, he went to discuss his predicament with Edwin Gooch, who lived in the same village. Edwin, the son of the local blacksmith, had just been elected as

Labour MP for North Norfolk in the 1945 landslide election. Edwin had been a founder member of the South Norfolk Labour Party when it was formed in Wymondham in 1918, and had been the agent for George Edwards (founder of the agricultural workers' union) when he was elected as MP for South Norfolk in 1920. Edwin had also been president of the National Union of Agricultural Workers since 1928 (a position he maintained until his death in 1964). By trade he was a journalist on the *Norwich Mercury*, and he used these skills in support of the cause of agricultural workers.

When Wilf told Edwin that he needed a job and wanted to help rebuild the country, Edwin advised him to see the Labour Party agent, Jock Watson, at his office in Wymondham. Jock, in turn, advised Wilf to join the agricultural workers' union and the Labour Party. Honest as ever, Wilf felt duty-bound to point out two minor obstacles to this: he was not an agricultural worker; and he was marxist, whereas the Labour Party was not. Jock reassured him on both counts. He explained that the union had to rely on people who were not farmworkers to be branch secretaries in many areas, because farmers would sack and evict any of their workers who took on these positions. It was quite often publicans that took on the role (and in Thaxted the vicar, Reverend Jack Putterill, chaired the branch). Even Edwin Gooch, the union's president, was a journalist. When Wilf stated his commitment to marxism as an obstacle to joining the Labour Party, Jock replied:

Don't worry. I was a marxist before the war, itching for the revolution that was going to put the country to rights, but now things have changed radically. We have a Labour government with a majority of 146, a government for the people, no compromises or backtracking like we experienced with Ramsay Macdonald in 1931. It'll be all onwards and upwards from now on, you'll see. And the AEU [Amalgamated Engineering Union] has got a resolution on the agenda of the Labour Party conference calling for the affiliation of the Communist Party … we shall have one huge working-class party, not divided between communists and labour.

In fact this resolution was to be heavily defeated at the 1946 conference, but Wilf accepted Jock's assurances and joined both the Labour Party and the agricultural workers' union.

He found that his experience as an RAF lecturer helped him to express himself when making public speeches in support of newly elected South Norfolk Labour MP Christopher Mayhew. The Oxford-educated Mayhew (son of a former High Sheriff of Norfolk) was very much a professional who got a polite reception, whereas Wilf had the common touch which established a deeper rapport with the audience, and he talked to them about their everyday concerns.

One day, when the two of them were travelling together to a meeting in the market town of Dereham, Wilf told the MP of his disquiet over the sending of British troops to Burma to fight Britain's former allies, who had helped defeat the Japanese but were now struggling for their independence. The response of Mayhew was: 'Oh, I don't know anything about the politics of foreign affairs.' Very soon after this statement he was made Under Secretary for Foreign Affairs! Wilf was astonished.

Wilf's public speaking impressed Edwin Gooch, who suggested that he should apply for the vacant job as his agent. Wilf was the only applicant for the position, but he was not given an easy ride by the six people interviewing him. One of them was an old socialist called Billy Pask, a tailor by trade, from Norwich. Billy asked him: 'If we appoint you as an agent

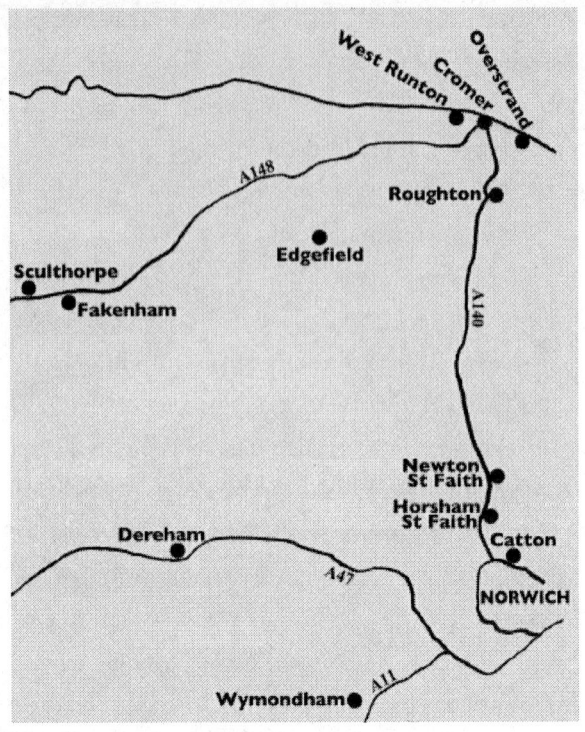

Map of North Norfolk showing some of the main places mentioned in the text

and you learn how to run elections and organise things, what's to stop you joining the Tory Party and getting a much higher salary than we can offer you later on?' To this Wilf replied: 'The only answer I can give you to that is that I'm a socialist.' Billy 'purred like a kitten' – and Wilf got the job. Another member of the interviewing panel was Arthur Amiss, who had taken part in the 1923 farm workers' strike against wage cuts. Arthur remembered Wilf as a very able worker, and later tried to persuade him against resigning from the party.

Agent to Edwin Gooch

After being told that he had been appointed to the job, a small detail was added: Wilf would receive no salary but would have to raise funds for his income from the branches, through activities such as whist drives. He managed to achieve this, however, after building up 20 new branches with up to 30 members in each.

The next urgent priority was to get housing for his young family; his parents' cottage, where the family were staying, was just too overcrowded. A temporary solution was a holiday home at West Runton on the north Norfolk coast, which they rented for a fixed period from October 1945 to Easter 1946. And because they could not find an affordable alternative at the end of this time, they carried on living in the house until served with a court order to quit.

Housing was desperately short after the war, because so much had been destroyed by bombing, and the rebuilding of council housing was slow to start, especially in rural areas. Squatting was one response to this problem, mainly in the towns and cities, and often organised by the Communist Party. And indeed squatting was a tactic that would be later used by Wilf to help farmworkers evicted from tied cottages. But at this point it did not seem to him a feasible solution to his own family's problem. Luck came to his rescue, however, just as he and his family were about to be evicted. By chance he met in Cromer a former comrade from the RAF, who told him of an old railway carriage – 'Treehaven', in nearby Roughton – that was for sale at a price of £200. This was beyond Wilf's pocket, but Lady Sanderson, a wealthy Labour Party member whose husband was the first principal of Ruskin college for trade unionists in Oxford, lent him the money.

The railway carriage was in a very dilapidated condition, having been unoccupied for more than six years. Brambles were growing all over the property, and the first task was to clear a path to the doorway. Worse still was the lack of amenities – no gas, no electricity, no water and no mains drainage. The family had to use oil lamps for lighting and bottles of gas for cooking and heating, and water had to be fetched from a distant standpipe. The toilet was an Elsan closet, the contents of which they had to bury in a pit. And the roof leaked, so that every time it rained they had to put out buckets and cans to collect the water. 'The different dripping sounds made it sound like music,' recalled Wilf's daughter Carol. All necessities had to be lugged from the village shop – which was more than a mile away – in all weathers. A compensation, however, was that the field next to the carriage was part of their land, so they were able to grow vegetables, keep chickens for eggs, and even have pigs and rabbits. This helped supplement their meagre income and allowed them to live healthily, if frugally. 'The goose and duck eggs were huge, filling the whole frying pan at breakfast,' remembered Carol. 'Dad brought us some piglets, which we had in our beds, but mother was furious when she found out.'

One major drawback was the distance the two children, Carol and John, had to walk to school – three miles. This was at a time before the widespread availability of school buses, and long before the family had a car; Wilf had to cycle around all the villages in his work as Labour agent. The school's headmaster once told Wilf that his children thought the world owed them a living: later they were both to become professors. When Carol was taking her 11-plus examination at Cromer primary school in 1952, she was told by her teacher that no daughter of a communist would ever go to a grammar school. Though she didn't pass the examination, she thrived in the secondary modern school, and, with the help of her parents, later went to City College in Norwich.

Carol remembers being taken for a walk by Wilf when she was a young child in the late 1940s:

He showed me a road being made up for a rich employer, just so his child could ride a bike on it. He pointed out that the farm workers who were building it could not afford to buy shoes for their children. He also took me to see a family being thrown out of their cottage and later to see them again after he got them a council home, and their faces lit up. It showed me that justice and peace had to be struggled for.

This was while Wilf was still working for Edwin Gooch, and looking for Labour candidates to stand in local elections in villages around the constituency. Because he could not get anyone to stand for the village of Edgefield, on the Erpingham Rural District Council, he stood himself and was elected. In this he was following in an honourable tradition: this was the council that George Edwards had served on to great effect. At the time when Erpingham council had been formed (after the District and Parish Councils Act of 1894) it had had six Labour representatives, which was the highest number for a rural area in the whole of England. George Edwards had been returned unopposed to Erpingham council in 1897, and had become chairman of its sanitary committee in 1900. Before leaving the council in 1910, he and his fellow councillors had made use of the Housing Act to build council houses for workers in Edgefield. And Edgefield was often visited by George when he was recruiting members to the agricultural workers' union in its early days. At one or two public meetings he had been knocked about a bit by farmworkers who thought he would upset the farmers, and after that he had always chosen to speak on top of a pile of stones – so that he was in control of the ammunition! This tactic was later recommended to budding union speakers by Bill Holmes, who was general secretary from 1928 to 1945.

Wilf was not one to incur expenses in his work. To save the

party travelling costs he had once hitch-hiked from Norfolk to Bournemouth for the annual Labour Party conference – only to be rebuked for undermining the expenses system. This had helped to make him suspicious of the bureaucracy. His job as Gooch's agent was very badly paid but he still tackled it with great relish, and got immense satisfaction from it. He set up many Labour Party branches in the villages, and these provided support for Gooch and ensured that the MP knew what his constituents wanted. About 98 per cent of the members were farmworkers: 'It was just after the war and they were all very enthusiastic about what was going to happen. I remember going into fields and they would gather round stacks to talk to me about what was happening, and they really appreciated that the Labour Party agent was there to see them.'

In building up a political movement in the villages, Wilf helped some of the parish councils to shake off their almost feudal dependency on the local squires. The council meetings were often held in the manor house of the squire, who was also frequently the chairman. After the transformation, meetings would be held in village halls, and squires would be voted off the council. Naturally, Wilf challenged the local squirearchy on his own Erpingham council. At his first meeting he was amazed to see that the chairman, Sir Henry Upcher, along with the vice-chairman and the clerk, decided between themselves which councillors would serve on the committees – which was where all the decisions were made. Only 20 out of the 52 councillors were allocated to committees, and this meant that all the real decisions were being made by a small clique:

This was the way it had always been, as nobody had wanted to rock the boat or fall out with Sir Henry. So I moved a proposition that all the committee positions should be filled by the full council electing them. This went through quite easily with no trouble at all, but it had to be from the following year.

When that time came around, Sir Henry proposed that 60 per cent of the committee positions should be elected by the full council, and 40 per cent by him and his two cronies, to ensure there was 'continuity'. Wilf spoke unsuccessfully against this compromise, but nevertheless was satisfied that he had made a significant advance.

He also insisted that councillors rather than staff would count the votes, and ended up being one of the counters himself.

Differences with the Labour Party

When the National Health Service was formed in 1948, Edwin Gooch introduced Wilf to health minister Nye Bevan and they got on well. Wilf was nominated by the Eastern Counties Federation of Trades Councils to serve on the Norfolk Executive Council of the NHS to help set up the service in the county, and this was approved by Nye. Wilf had a heated argument with Nye on one occasion, however, over the drug companies. Wilf foresaw that they would be allowed to charge what they liked for the drugs they supplied, and would therefore be able to cream off money from the health service – unless measures were taken to control them. Nye's response was to tell Wilf not to worry: 'I've got my eye on it, but at the moment the doctors are refusing to come in. Let's deal with that first.'

The Minister of Agriculture, Tom Williams, was another member of the government tackled by Wilf. In 1947 the minister gave security of tenure to small farmers. (Up until then their leases had expired every Michaelmas, and the landowners often evicted them after they had built up their farms). Wilf went to see the minister and argued that as well as giving security of tenure to farmers he should also give it to farmworkers. The minister replied: 'I can't do that. If you give them security of tenure you've got to give the policeman security of tenure in his police house even if he is sacked or wants to leave. And what about the prime minister in 10 Downing Street? Is he going to stay there if he loses the next election?' Wilf's response was that this was 'a load of codswallop' – but to no avail.

Wilf was also at odds with the leadership on the way council house building was being financed. At the Labour Party conference Norwich Constituency Labour Party had moved that interest-free loans should be made for this purpose. But this motion was not acted upon, and financiers subsequently made fortunes in loaning money to the councils at high interest rates, which slowed down the rebuilding programme. Wilf also disagreed with the Labour leadership over the form that nationalisation took: 'I opposed it because it wasn't putting the industries into the hands of the people, but into the hands of bureaucratic boards'.

He was also opposed to the Labour government's actions in sending troops to Korea, Malaya and Indonesia, as well as Burma. One day, when Wilf was selling the *Daily Worker* door to door in Holt, a man whose son was serving in Korea unleashed his Alsatian dog on him. 'It was a vicious dog that would have torn me to pieces,' said Wilf. 'So I leapt over the fence and jumped into my car, from where I shouted that I did not want his son to risk his life in Korea.'

In 1949 Wilf decided that he could no longer accept the policies that were being introduced by the Labour government, and he resigned as Edwin Gooch's agent. An organiser was sent to try and persuade Wilf to change his mind, with the promise of future rewards. 'Hang on to the job,' he advised. 'Gooch is getting older. We'll get you a job in the union as an organiser, then you can take over as president, and become MP for North Norfolk when he retires.' But Wilf was not to be persuaded. 'I was seen as Gooch's protégé, so there was tremendous pressure on me to stay in,' he recalled. 'But I couldn't do it because it would not have been loyal to the people who were paying me.'

As he put it in his letter of resignation: 'I regret that the differences between the Labour Party leaders and myself are affecting my efficiency. I had hoped that this chasm would have been merely temporary. It is obvious however that the gulf is widening. I have therefore no alternative but to submit my resignation as a paid official of the Labour Party.' He later explained the reasons more fully, and they were set out in Bob Wynn's *Skilled At All Trades, The history of the farmworkers' union 1947-1984* (see bibliography): 'I objected to the way the Labour Government was smashing up the resistance movements in countries like Greece and Malaya, fighting the very people who had fought on our side during the war. Then came the Marshall Plan which subjected Britain to US domination. It was too much, so I resigned.'

Edwin Gooch was so upset by his resignation that he did not speak to Wilf for two years afterwards. Then they met by chance walking in Cromer, and Wilf congratulated Edwin on his stand on the Labour Party National Executive against German rearmament. 'We didn't lose all those men in the war to have it start all over again, my boy,' replied Edwin, and the two became close friends again.

6. Blacklisted communist

I n 1950 the *Daily Worker* carried an ad announcing that Wilf's old RAF comrade Dan Cohen needed to replace his election agent (who had been injured in a car accident), to run his campaign as the Communist Party candidate at Paddington North in the general election of 23 February. Wilf applied for the job and got it.

This was a period of highly publicised spy trials, which had led to the general portrayal of all communists as traitors. In Britain Klaus Fuchs had been jailed for giving nuclear secrets to the Soviet Union, while in the USA Ethel and Julius Rosenberg had been electrocuted for similar charges – which they denied to the end. Unperturbed, Wilf arranged a series of public meetings at three local schools, at each of which Dan Cohen was well received. But in spite of a good campaign, Cohen lost his deposit. His 417 votes amounted to 1.15 per cent of the total (though this was four times the average percentage for communists, and he was also competing against a Socialist

Party of Great Britain candidate). In total, Communist candidates across the country received 91,765 votes, which was 0.3 per cent of the total.

Labour received 13,266,176 votes (46.1 per cent) and 315 seats, while the Conservatives got 11,507,061 votes (40 per cent) and 282 seats. The other parties won 37 seats, including three for the Independent Labour Party, which meant that it only needed one ILP member to voted against Labour for it to lose its majority. This lack of an overall majority led Labour to call another general election the following year. But this time, though Labour increased its support to 13,948,883 (48.8 per cent), and the Conservatives vote decreased to 12,660,061 (44.3 per cent), the Conservatives nevertheless won the election, with 302 seats compared to Labour's 295.

In spite of the small vote, Wilf had found working with his former mentor extremely fulfilling, and he was so impressed with the integrity and sincerity of his fellow comrades that he decided to join the Communist Party. This presented a potential problem with his Edgefield seat on Erpingham rural district council, where he had sat as a Labour Party member since 1947, and where he was now due for re-election. Wilf (who had by now moved to Overstrand) therefore raised the matter with the Edgefield members: 'I was very worried about it, but they rallied round and actually stopped the Labour Party putting up a candidate against me because they thought I was doing a tremendous job for them'.

As a result of this, Wilf was returned as a communist councillor in every election from then until 1974. He even managed to get elected to Norfolk county council too, in so doing beating the Conservative candidate Major A.R. Gurney, a wealthy farmer from Northrepps (just south of Overstrand). The major had always previously lent his lawn mower to the local football club for cutting the grass on their pitch. But his election defeat by a communist so rankled that when the club next asked to borrow the mower he refused, saying 'you might ask Mr Wilfred Page if he has got one'. (At other times, however, Wilf and the Major had a good working relationship – and this was also the case with John Kumar, the chair of the North Norfolk Farmers.)

Many of Wilf's successes as a councillor involved preventing evictions of agricultural workers from tied cottages, or getting them rehoused. In 1950 one of these cases was reported in the *Country Standard*, the communist journal for rural workers. The journal gave credit to Wilf for having delayed the eviction of a Southrepps farm worker and his family – including a three-week-old baby – until he had managed to secure them a council house. This outraged the agricultural workers' union, which denounced him in its journal *The Landworker* (September 1950), under the heading 'Communist Misrepresentation'. This was Wilf's first ever mention in his own union's journal – and he was accused of 'endeavouring to deceive the unwary and cause them to think that Communists are the only, or at least the most effective, fighters on behalf of the workers.' The *Landworker* was to attack the *Country Standard* on a further occasion in September 1952, under the heading 'Communist Offensive'. The crime this time was the journal's criticism of a Labour Party pamphlet *Our Daily Bread*, because it had not pledged legislation against tied cottage evictions. The *Landworker* warned readers that Communism was an 'unscrupulous and cynical fraud'.

When Wilf decided to stand for election as secretary of the union's Roughton branch, the editor of the *Landworker*, along with others from central office, came down to the meeting to dissuade members from voting for him. Wilf subsequently lost the election by just one vote, but the successful candidate didn't stay long in the job, and a few months later Wilf was asked to take over.

Local battles

Some of Wilf's tactics for preventing workers from being made homeless were quite imaginative, and they were almost always effective. On one occasion, he enlisted the support of the local bishop in the case of a farmworker from Little Barningham who had been threatened with eviction after injuring his back when falling off a haycart. After several weeks in hospital the farmworker was released, on condition that he perform only light duties for a while and return to hospital twice a week for physiotherapy treatment. On hearing this his employer told him: 'If you think I am going to pay you a farm worker's wage to do a light job and let you go on this new fangled electricity treatment twice a week you have got another think coming.' The next day the accident victim received in the post two letters, one terminating his employment and the other giving him notice to vacate his house.

Wilf tried unsuccessfully to help the family find a council house, but there was none available. He did not give up the battle however. He remembered a talk on the Christian Marxist dialogue he had given not long before, to a group of parsons in the village of Horstead:

> I had told them that they were behind manse walls when it came to really important problems facing their villagers. Afterwards I thought this was very unkind to them. So now I thought I would challenge the church to help in this case, and got in touch with the Bishop of Norwich to help this lad and

his family to avoid being thrown out of their home. The bishop referred me to his industrial chaplain, Rev Michael Mann.

I took him in the pouring rain to their little cottage, knocked on the door and walked in. The door opened into the living room where an old lady was kneeling by the fireplace and praying and begging God that he wouldn't allow her furniture to be thrown out into the pelting rain and get ruined. The family told Rev Mann the whole story and he was terribly distressed by it. Less than a week later the family phoned me to let me know that they had got a council house. It was quite evident that the Bishop's office had got in touch with some of the landed gentry who were on the council and paved the way for our member to be rehoused.

Never one to miss a recruiting opportunity, Wilf went on to persuade Rev Mann to join a union and to attend his trades council as a delegate from the church. (Wilf's close friend, blacksmith Mike Ward, suspected Wilf might have stage-managed the praying in advance, but Wilf was adamant that this was not what had happened.) Some years later Wilf was to read the lesson at a harvest festival service in Norwich Cathedral, representing the union. He explained his views thus: 'The Bible says love thy neighbour as thyself, and the Union says an injury to one is an injury to all.'

In another case, a farm worker near Wymondham was being evicted from his house because his employer had objected to him building a garage for his car in the garden. Because he was not a member, the union had refused to take the case, but had suggested that Wilf might support him in court. However one of the court flunkies told Wilf that he would not be allowed to represent the worker, because he was not a solicitor. Wilf was not one to back down, and made it clear that he was not leaving – eventually being allowed in. He told the Judge: 'if I had known about this case a few weeks ago when the farmer was making his threats I would have had him in court for unfair dismissal'. To which the judge replied: 'Not in this court, my boy, you wouldn't.' But Wilf must have made

an impression, because the judge went on to rule against the farmer, and he also granted security of tenure to the farm worker. 'It was the only case that was ever won for absolute tenure. So we went and had a drink and I asked why he wasn't in the bloody union, after which he joined, and became an activist, attending a rally in Great Yarmouth.'

A few weeks later the same farmer asked to see Wilf about the case, so Wilf and the farm worker went to his manor house:

> We went into this huge baronial room where he plied us with whisky and said he wanted us to go back to court and this time lose the case – but in return he would make sure the lad got a council house through friends of his on the council. I thought bugger that, so we rejected the idea. But we carried on drinking whisky until about 10 o'clock at night, by which time we had consumed about a bottle and a half between us.

Driving home I thought, I bet that bugger's got me drunk and has rung the police to say there is someone driving under the influence of drink. And when I went past the police station in Wymondham a coppers' car followed me. But they lost me when I went left instead of straight on. I still think it was a put-up job.

Another case involved a heavily pregnant woman, Mrs Wright, who was due to give birth in two days' time, and had been told to quit her tied cottage in Northrepps six days after that. Wilf consulted his friend Herbert Harvey, a union member and fellow councillor, and the two of them went to the council housing officer, only to be told no housing was available. At this Herbert's clenched fist hammered the office table, frightening the life out of the officer, who said he would see what could be done. As a result they managed to get Mrs Wright keys to an unfinished house, before it was officially ready for occupation. The boiler in the kitchen and the fireplace in the living room had still to be installed. When they pointed out that there were no cooking facilities yet, she replied that she did not have them in the house from which she was being evicted. The family stayed in the living room until the building workers had finished off the house.

Housing was always one of Wilf's major concerns, and he put forward a motion at the local council that it should adopt the powers of the Housing Requisitioning Act, which enabled the council to lend money to people to buy their houses. As the moustache of chairman Sir Henry Upcher twitched, Wilf knew he was furious at the suggestion. 'Mr Page,' he snorted, 'councils are not responsible for finance outside their own work. That is the job of money lenders.' Undeterred, Wilf pointed out that rural workers didn't want to get into the clutches of money

Daily Worker cartoons by Gabriel attacking the government for cutting spending on housing and increasing it on arms shortly after the 1951 election (published on 3 Nov and 17 Dec). Santa Mac was Harold Macmillan, Minister of Housing.

"You'll observe, of course, that there has been some modifications to your original request"

"Ssh! Just a little alteration to our election programme!"

lenders, in case they hit hard times and were not able to keep up the payments. He argued that if the council loaned the money it could help people at times of difficulty. Another councillor, a captain, expressed his wrath at the idea: 'I've had enough of these Comintern tactics,' he fumed. 'Mr Page should go to Russia if he wants to bring these kinds of things in. We're not having it!' Wilf struck back: 'Well, I'm surprised at the captain saying this ... because this Act was passed in 1886 during the reign of Queen Victoria, and no-one could accuse her of being a buxom bolshevik could they?' The whole council broke into uproarious laughter and voted to adopt the powers of the Act. 'You can win them over if you make them laugh,' commented Wilf.

Wilf's knowledge of housing legislation on one occasion helped a farm worker to gain a government subsidy to build his own bungalow:

> I was on the housing committee and was looking through some acts of parliament when I came across the Financial and Miscellaneous Act. This gave twenty-year subsidies for houses being built in the interests of agriculture. It did not say this was only for farm owners, but it was them who were making use of it to build new houses all over the place with the subsidy. So I got a constituent of mine, a farm worker, who wanted to build his own bungalow to make an application. He eventually got the grant and was the only example I knew of a worker who got it.

The worker in question was Billy Bunting, who lived in Edgefield, and whom Wilf had first met when he was addressing the unemployed in a dole queue in Cromer. He had told the people in the queue that there were plenty of unused bricks in Peterborough, and people needed houses, and yet those who could build them were out of work: 'As a communist I disapprove of this waste.' Billy was in the queue and became one of Wilf's supporters, along with his son Vic, a cowman.

Another of Wilf's supporters was Ray Bunting, who had been born in 1927 in one of the council houses built in the time of George Edwards. Ray's father had been in the 1923 farm workers' strike, and had run the union's Edgefield branch, which had more than one hundred members, meeting in the King's Head in Holt. Ray's parents had also run the local Labour Party, but, according to Ray, 'they accepted Wilf's opinion when he left Labour because they thought he was still a champion of working-class people. His vote did not go down when he joined the Communist Party.' Ray remembered Wilf at one time winning the seat against his boss at the gravel pit where he worked. Wilf was also the photographer at Ray's wedding in 1949. The ceremony was conducted by the local vicar, Rev Grainger, a Labour Party member who caused a stir when he said that Christ was the first communist. Ray's wife was the Edgefield postwoman, and she used to pass on any problems she heard about on her rounds to Wilf. After sorting out the letters in her kitchen she delivered them by bicycle. A strong member of the postal workers' union, she duly went on strike when it was called – on her own, in the village.

Another of Wilf's successes on the council was to get a dustcart collection to cover all the villages in the district. At first this had been rejected on grounds of cost. But then Wilf pointed out that villagers were resorting to throwing rubbish into the hedgerows, which was attracting rats. This struck a cord with the farmers on the council, who were worried that the rats would eat their corn. Suddenly all cost objections were dropped and another victory was achieved.

The tribulations of work

Although Wilf invested immense amounts of time and effort into his work as a councillor, such work did not pay the bills (there were not the generous expenses that can now be paid to councillors). So he was always looking for work, which was not an easy task for someone of his widely known politics.

After leaving his job with the Labour Party he had been lucky enough to become a lecturer for the extra-mural board of studies in Cambridge: 'I lectured on government and parliamentary procedures in various army camps to lads about to leave the forces, telling them about how local councils worked. I got well paid for that, but it did not last for long. I lost it when somebody at Cambridge was found spying for the Soviet Union.'

After this Wilf was a lorry driver for a while, then after the 1953 floods on the east coast he got work repairing the sea defences. In the summer he tried to earn a few shillings as a beach photographer. He and Christina also ran a clifftop cafe in Overstrand for a time, but because he did not charge anyone who was hungry they did not make a great commercial success of it.

Hopes of a permanent job were raised when Wilf heard that a new intensive turkey unit was opening in Northrepps, and a manager was needed:

> The owner asked me what I knew about turkeys, and I said not much, but I knew they would need a careful systematic approach and be fed properly or they would get disease; and that I was familiar with working on systematic schemes in the forces. So he said to come along on Monday. On the Monday I set off, expecting to start work, with my marmalade sandwiches which my missus had made. When I got there he said: 'You really want a job don't you?' I said 'yes' and he replied: 'Well go to bloody Russia and get one.' I was bitterly disappointed at this viciousness, but it did not weaken my principles, it strengthened them.

When it came to blacklisting Wilf was more accustomed to being given a job on Friday and then finding it had mysteriously disappeared by the following Monday (after the employer had checked him out on the telephone). Even when he did avoid the blacklist and find a job it would not be long before Wilf was organising his workmates and getting victimised for this – and getting sacked again. One example of this was when he worked at a sugar beet processing factory and campaigned for and won protective boots for the workers. After that he got them into the union – and found himself back on the stones.

A more spectacular example of dismissal ended his brief career as a bus driver in Cromer in 1955, which he began shortly after he had passed his Public Service Vehicle driving test in April of that year. Wilf had discovered that Eastern Counties buses were planning to get rid of conductors and make the drivers collect fares as passengers came on board. Wilf, like many workers and passengers, did not agree with this. And after he joined the company as a driver he managed to unionise the workforce and stop the introduction of driver-only buses, much to the annoyance of the employers.

Then an unfortunate accident occurred. One day Wilf had dropped off fifty schoolchildren from a double-decker bus at Suffield Park and was getting ready for the return trip to the centre of Cromer. He thought it would be dangerous to turn the bus round with so many children standing by the road, and so decided to keep going forward and to take a different route back. This route took him under the railway bridge in Station Road at Suffield Park, but sadly it was a low bridge, and the upper deck of the bus was torn off. The local paper cautiously reported that the omnibus 'came in contact with' the bridge – just in case the bridge was the guilty party. Headlined 'Upper Deck of Bus Crushed at Cromer', this press cutting was kept by Wilf in his scrapbook for the rest of his life. Wilf's hand was cut by broken glass in the accident, but his bosses had no sympathy for him at all. Instead they seized upon the incident as a pretext to sack him once more.

Luckily Christina was working for the county council's dental treatment service at this time, and her wages helped to keep the wolf from the door. But she had to give this job up when, having been elected to take part in a union delegation to Romania, she was refused leave to go on it.

George Edwards addressing Norfolk agricultural workers on strike
in 1923, courtesy *Landworker*

Strikers' banner, Mulbarton branch of the National Union of Agricultural
Labourers and Rural Workers, courtesy National Museum of Labour History

Above left Joseph Arch, founder of the first national agricultural workers' union in 1872, and MP for North West Norfolk from 1885 to 1900

Above right Wilf's grandfather, William Page

Billy and Alice Page, Wilf's parents, on their wedding day in 1912

Above left Wilf and family in 1922. Wilf is seated at the front, Doreen is standing right (next to grandfather Thomas Randall), Vera Alice is on Alice's lap, and Billy is standing at the back

Above right Family outing to the seaside about 1925: Wilf with his sisters (from the top) Doreen, Vera Alice and Sylvia

Wilf as a servant at the age of 15 in 1928

Wilf as an aerial photographer in the RAF in India in the 1930s

Wilf with Edwin Gooch in the late 1940s

Wilf has a lone admirer on the hustings in the 1950s

Addressing a slightly larger gathering

Working as a tractor driver in the 1960s

Playing Santa in 1957 at the British-Czech Friendship Society
Christmas party in Cromer. Christina is holding a baby on the right.
Courtesy Norfolk News Co

Wilf (left) marches with TUC general secretary Len Murray (right) at the
annual rally of the agricultural workers' union at Great Yarmouth in 1974.
Courtesy Eastern Counties Newspapers

Wilf chairs the agricultural trade group of the TGWU South East and East Anglia region in 1984. Chris Kaufman (then *Landworker* editor and now national secretary of Unite rural and agricultural workers) is in the back row, far right. Next to him is Tony Gould (later senior regional organiser for the TGWU rural and agricultural workers in East Anglia and the South East. © Andrew Wiard

Wilf and Christina with her TUC gold badge in 1979, courtesy
Mark Rusher, IFL

Wilf receives a Tolpuddle platter from Ian Gibson in 1984. Courtesy
Eastern Counties Newspapers

Shaking hands with fellow protester Peter Melchett at the perimeter fence at USAF base Sculthorpe. Courtesy *Country Standard*

With Bert Hazell, former president of the agricultural workers' union, at a pensioners rally at Norwich City football ground in 1989 © Peter Everard Smith

Wilf receiving his TGWU gold badge from Ron Todd in 1986. Jack Boddy (national secretary of the agricultural group) is pictured left, and Christina, right.

Addressing Norwich TGWU retired members' association conference in 1987 with guest Margaret Beckett
© Peter Everard Smith

Pensioners' rally, Norwich City football ground 1991
© Peter Everard Smith

With the Rev Canon Colin Beswick at Norwich cathedral, where Wilf read the lesson at the 1986 Harvest Thanksgiving service – taking a tractor to represent the farm workers' contribution © Peter Everard Smith

On the platform at the Burston Strike School rally in 1991, with Labour MP Denis Skinner (speaking), Ian Gibson (left) and international delegate Carlos Allones © Peter Everard Smith

Receiving a crystal decanter in 1998 from TGWU retired members' association president Jack Jones, courtesy T&G *Record*

Selling the *Anglian Pensioner* in his electric wheelchair at a rally in
Swaffham in 1998, with retired T&G general secretary Moss Evans (left),
who settled in Norfolk and became mayor of Kings Lynn and West Norfolk
in 1996; branch secretary Brian Mattins is pushing the wheelchair
© Peter Everard Smith

With daughter Carol at the Burston rally in 1998
© Peter Everard Smith

7. Union and community activist

By the mid-1950s Wilf was president both of Erpingham Rural District Tenants' Association, and of Cromer and District Trades Council (the latter position being taken up by Christina some years later). In these roles Wilf received constant coverage in the local press, especially for the campaigns he led against rent rises and against rising unemployment (both of which he blamed on high interest charges). Despite this, he was being frozen out by the leadership of his own trade union. He was variously chairman and secretary of the Roughton branch of the National Union of Agricultural Workers, but was constantly rejected from attending union schools, always being told that all the places had been taken. After he had been turned down for the seventh year in succession (in 1960, when he had just become secretary of the East Anglian committee of the Communist Party), the North Norfolk district organiser of the union, Jack Wilson, wrote in protest to the general secretary Harold Collison:

It is pretty obvious to me and to members of the North Walsham District Committee that Bro. Page is being excluded because of his political views. He is an active chairman of his branch, whose meetings are very properly conducted and benefit from his stewardship. As is obvious from Biennial Election ballots he commands the support and respect of quite a large number of members.

This continual exclusion of Bro. Page from one of the benefits and services of union membership is causing me and other members deep concern. It is obviously contrary to twice declared decisions of the Biennial Conference of the Union [against banning communists] … and I as a democrat am most perturbed at this discrimination.

Incidentally, I feel sure that other members attending the school would benefit from his presence in that he obviously has the ability to make positive contributions to the various discussions.

I think we are vastly underestimating the level of intelligence and the calibre of those other students if we think that Bro. Page would be able to undermine their beliefs during his short stay at the school.

Obviously he has a point of view which he feels bound to put over, but I have found no evidence at all that other members with whom he is constantly in contact accept his political opinions. They like his personality and appreciate the work that he is always prepared to put in on their behalf.

Jack had even visited the school and found there was room for four more people on it – though Wilf had been told it was fully booked.

It appeared that the protest had been heeded when, in November 1962, Wilf was surprised to receive a letter from the general secretary Harold Collison, inviting him to attend the union school in Clacton-on-Sea in January 1963. Payments for loss of wages and railway travel were promised. Wilf's delight was short-lived, however: in the same month he received another letter cancelling the invitation. Collison explained that it had been sent in error, and that 'the Executive Committee had previously decided that in view of your considerable knowledge of union affairs no invitation could be given'. He was being rejected for having too much knowledge of the union! In reply Wilf observed: 'The reasons you give do not appear to be very well founded. I would have thought it desirable to have present students at all levels to ensure the school's success.'

In spite of these difficulties, Wilf was elected to the biennial conferences of the union every two years from 1952 onwards. 1952 was also the year he stood for the union's executive committee for the first time, but it was to take seventeen more years before he finally succeeded. The prejudice he had to overcome could be seen in a motion passed at the 1955 North Norfolk conference of the union, that 'no member of the union who is a communist or has communist sympathies should be allowed to hold any office in the union'. This motion was not adopted nationally, however.

Cultural activities

Wilf's conduct of branch meetings, which had so impressed his area organiser, included the reading of a different chapter of the *Ragged Trousered Philanthropists* at the start of each one (this was Robert Tressell's classic novel that exposed and explained the exploitation of workers). He was also an enthusiast for a wide range of other cultural activities, and this was one reason for his popularity.

> I formed a youth club in Overstrand and organised evenings
> of one-act plays. Then I got in touch with the parish councils
> and told them we could put plays on for them to raise funds
> for their village halls where we staged them. These would
> attract farm workers and others into the audience, and they
> saw I was not the nasty type that they had imagined. I had
> built up a lot of support doing this, so when the right wing in
> the union attacked me some of these people would say they
> had met me raising money for their village hall with the youth
> club, and I was a good bloke.

Through the Cromer Co-operative Guild, Wilf and Christina also organised visits by the Unity Mobile Theatre Company, which put on plays such as *The Rochdale Pioneers* by James R Gregson, about the growth of the early co-operative movement. For one performance, in October 1953, they hired the Regal Cinema in Cromer, and two coachloads of people came from Norwich to watch it. Many years later the agit-prop theatre group 7:84 put on a performance about the Tolpuddle Martyrs in Norwich, and this time people took coaches from Cromer to see it.

Wilf was also a lover of folk music. Folk singers Ewan MacColl and Peggy Seeger stayed with Wilf and Christina in 1959 when they were researching a programme about herring fishermen on the east coast, part of a series called *Radio Ballads* which was broadcast in 1960.

Sam Larner was recorded singing 'Up jumped the herring' in his home at Winterton-on-Sea. Sam, who was born in 1878, had first gone to sea at the age of eight, and had become a cabin boy at the age of 12 on a sailing lugger fishing for herring in the North Sea – 'when we left school it was sea or jail for us'. He stayed at sea in all weathers for over forty years, until he was made unemployed during the depression of the 1930s.

Ewan MacColl wrote a song for the programme based on Sam's life, called 'Shoals of Herring':

> Oh, it was a fine and a pleasant day
> Out of Yarmouth harbour I was faring
> As a cabin boy on a sailing lugger
> For to go and hunt the shoals of herring.
> …
>
> In the stormy seas and the living gale
> Just to earn your daily bread you're daring
> From the Dover Straits to the Faroe Islands
> While you're following the shoals of herring.

Another song on the programme was 'Singing the Fishing', sung by Yarmouth fisherman Ronnie Balls, who added: 'If you fish for the herring, they rule your life.'

MacColl's 'Shoals of Herring' became the best-known of all the songs from the radio series, and was recorded by many other groups, including the Spinners and the Clancy Brothers. In Ireland it was adapted to become 'The Shores of Erin' – leading many to the false conclusion that MacColl's song was based on a traditional Irish song, though in fact it was the other way round.

'Shoals of Herring' became a particular favourite of Wilf's and it was played at his funeral.

Farmworkers'
VIEWPOINT
by Wilf Page

Our special correspondent recently visited one of the latest countries to join the EEC.

Wilf's byline in the Eastern Daily Press

Another of Wilf's ventures was a fortnightly column in the large circulation *Eastern Daily Press* entitled 'Farmworkers' Viewpoint'. This lasted from 1963 until 1976. He used the column to cover all manner of topics, including wages, housing, the common agricultural policy and land distribution. A constant theme was the high interest rates that councils had to pay in order to finance house building. In June 1965 he wrote:

> With local government work being mainly of a social character, they should not be subject to the fluctuations of the money market but should be able to raise loans with central government at very low interest charges. It seems quite preposterous that a council wishing to build a council house should have to borrow money at six per cent over 60 years and pay £7,425 for a £2,000 house.

As he pointed out in another column, when Erpingham rural district council borrowed £75,000 to build 28 bungalows, this meant it would ultimately have to pay another £200,000 in interest. And this would lead to increases in all council housing rents to meet the debt, which in turn would restrict the council's ability to build more houses. Wilf therefore called on the new Labour government to honour its election pledge to reduce interest rates on money borrowed by local authorities.

Peace and international friendship

Christina, who had stood as a communist candidate at Overstrand in the 1956 local elections, was a strong internationalist. She visited Czechoslovakia in 1957 as part of a Pilgrimage to Lidice, marking the fifteenth anniversary of the destruction of that small village near Prague by the Nazis in June 1942. As a reprisal for the killing of one of their officers, the Nazis had shot all males over the age of fifteen, sent all the women to concentration camps, and dispersed all the children throughout Germany. A rose garden in their memory was opened at which Christina was present. (Christina was also a union activist. In 1959 she was elected to the Southern and Eastern divisional council of her union, the Union of Shop, Distributive, and Allied Workers (USDAW) with 9,162 votes.)

Wilf took a party of children of Deal coalminers to Czechoslovakia in the same year, organised through Progressive Tours, the British communist travel agency. But even here Wilf's activism came into play: 'there was quite a shamozzle when we were put in a low level cheap area of Prague and just given sandwiches. Even though they were tough kids they resented being given the crumbs from the master's table as they saw it. But we sorted that out and there was a complete transformation after a few days.'

Wilf mentioned this trip to John Gotts when he was working with him in a sugar beet field. John played for Gimingham football club, and this gave the two of them the idea that the club could tour Czechoslovakia in the interests of international understanding. Wilf and Christina approached the Czech authorities with the suggestion, and the country's Sports Department agreed to finance a tour the following year; and the club subsequently played five matches there. In the same year a branch of the British Czechoslovak Friendship League was set up in Cromer, which had a successful Christmas party in St John Hall, with Wilf dressed-up as Santa Claus. Mike Ward recalled that Wilf and Christina organised holidays for Czech children in Norfolk, and managed to obtain a lot of bicycles for them. Years later, when the cycles were rusty and damaged, Wilf got Mike to repair them and they were sold for funds towards the *Country Standard*. 'They were very persuasive at getting people involved,' remarked Mike.

Wilf had first visited Czechoslovakia as part of a trade union delegation organised by the British Czechoslovak Friendship League in 1953, when he had visited co-operative farms:

Before the war about a million and a half smallholders farmed under 25 acres each, living on the verge of bankruptcy. It had only needed a long illness to bring disaster on the family. Village life was hard and poor. It was only possible to change over from individual small-scale farming to large-scale socialist farming along the lines of co-operatives. I met some of these farmers who voluntarily pooled their land and light machinery. They explained that it was the attractive contracts offered by the government which convinced them to work as a team rather than individually. They stressed the importance of the machine stations from which they hire heavy machinery and operators to do the bulk of the work on the farm. Three young men from the farm we visited were away at an agricultural college studying agricultural science and their fellow farmers were looking forward to their return with new ideas.

Wilf was also impressed by the equal pay for women agricultural workers, and the creches where they could leave their children while working on the farm. Another memorable moment was the bath he took in a room which had once been used by King Edward VI – and was now part of a health centre for workers run by the trade unions.

Wilf and Christina's daughter Carol was also able to go to a Czech international camp in the mid-1950s, when she was a young teenager. Over the years Wilf picked up enough of the Czech language to act as interpreter for a party of 29 Czech farmers who much later visited Norfolk, during the icy winter of 1981.

One breakthrough for international friendship came in 1958, when Wilf spoke at the union's national conference in favour of exchange visits with the Soviet Union, to increase goodwill and understanding between the nations. The motion was passed.

These initiatives for international friendship were taking place in the middle of the cold war. In 1958 Britain signed an agreement with the USA to build 15 nuclear missile bases in the UK, including five in East Anglia. The range of the missiles was 1,500 miles, which meant they could reach Soviet targets. Many people were against the missile bases because they realised they would make them a target for the other side. Fear of a nuclear war heightened, and the Campaign for Nuclear Disarmament (CND) was formed later in that year.

International peace was an issue about which both Wilf and Christina were passionate, and they were active in forming the Cromer CND group, of which Wilf was elected chairman. The group got a boost when an American spy plane (U2) was shot down over Russia in May, 1960 – and East Anglian links were revealed. The Americans originally claimed that the plane was a 'weather plane', thinking that both it and pilot had been destroyed. Then the Russians produced the pilot, Gary Powers, who admitted he had been on a spying mission. It was reported that papers from a Norwich jeweller were found on Powers, and that the plane had been tested over the previous four years at Lakenheath USAF base in Suffolk. Wilf, who took part in a protest march at Lakenheath, highlighted the dangers of East Anglia becoming targeted by the Russians in self defence as a result of all this. He also brought these issues into his speech in support of nuclear disarmament at the 1970 conference of the agricultural workers' union.

At least the matter was debated in 1970. At a previous union conference, the leadership had continually pushed nuclear disarmament further down the agenda. On the last day of the conference Wilf had demanded that it be debated. The president – Edwin Gooch – decided to appeal to the delegates' stomachs rather than rational argument: 'You have all got jolly good digs and I am sure your landladies have been slaving over stoves to cook a nice meal for you,' he said. 'If we spend time on this motion your meals will be spoiled.' His argument proved compelling enough for the delegates to vote against debating the issue.

Earning a crust

During the 1960s Wilf carried on working in many different jobs. He worked for a year on a county council smallholding of 60 acres in Gimingham. Then he went on to become an attendant on a caravan site in the small seaside village of Mundesley, just along the coast from Overstrand, where Christina worked in an old people's home. Here he tamed two pigeons to perch on his shoulder, and when one of them was run over the other became permanently attached to Wilf.

For a while Wilf sold fish from an old van touring around local villages. 'It was not refrigerated, so it stunk really badly,' recalled Carol. 'He used to buy the fish from the fisherman on the beach at Overstrand and then hawk them in the villages – while trying to sell the *Daily Worker* and recruit people to the Communist Party at the same time.' In one place where he was delivering there was a vicious Alsatian dog loose in the garden, so he simply threw the fish over the fence and scarpered.

Wilf's driving could be reckless at times. One day, for example, Wilf's son John broke down in his tiny three-wheel car, about fifty miles from home. Wilf asked the then union district organiser, Jack Boddy, to take him in his car to help him tow the three-wheeler back home. On the way back Wilf drove Jack's car, while Jack was persuaded to steer the broken-down vehicle as it was being towed along. The speed with which Wilf tore round the bends caused Jack to wave frantically at him the whole way, signalling that he should slow down. 'At the end he was a mixture of white with fear and red with rage,' recalled Carol.

Wilf's next job was with John Laing, mixing cement to help increase the length of the runways at Coltishall aerodrome. This paid good money, but only lasted for about six months. The company then employed him to drive lorries from Coltishall to Yeovil, returning by train. He did this so successfully that he was offered the position of transport foreman. But this would have involved being away from home a good deal, and Wilf therefore turned it down. Later, however, the need for money forced him to take a job driving lorries all over the country with a cowboy firm, whose lorries often had ineffective brakes. He also worked for a while on delivering greenhouses for Ernie Fulcher.

In 1962 Wilf's father Billy died, at the age of 78. The obituary in the local paper showed he had had as varied a list of jobs as his son – rag and bone man (using 'many varied temperamental donkeys and mules' to haul his carts), horse dealing, general shop owner, and seller of fish and chips, ice cream, rock, antiques, curios, second-hand furniture and donkeys. He had also played darts for the Queen's Head in Wymondham, where he had lived from 1928 onwards, it reported. (Wilf's favourite pub in Wymondham was The Green Dragon, judging from a birthday card it sent to him.)

In 1964, the year that Harold Wilson's first Labour government was elected after thirteen years of Tory rule, Wilf was a gardener. This was also the year in which he was finally accepted by the union to attend its winter school. And in the same year Christina was elected on to the national executive of USDAW, representing its 56,000 members in the Eastern Division. She was about as popular with her national union leadership as Wilf was with his – but she battled on relentlessly.

8. The national arena

arold Wilson's Labour government of 1964-1970 had many battles with the trade unions, and pay restraint, under its various guises, was one of the major issues. In 1965 the government announced legislation to back up its Prices and Incomes policy, whereby price increases and wage claims had to be referred to the Prices and Incomes Board (PIB) for approval. The following year it announced a pay freeze for lower paid workers. This meant that pay awards to agricultural workers could potentially be vetoed by the government.

In 1966 agricultural workers were awarded an increase of just six shillings (30p) a week by the Agricultural Wages Board (the government body that decides minimum pay and conditions annually after submissions from employers and unions), and this brought the standard rate up to £10 16s (£10.80) a week.[1] The union was confident that this would be within the government's limits, and was therefore appalled when the government referred the award to the Prices and Incomes

Board – though it was subsequently relieved to find that the
AWB increase was confirmed. Then in 1967 an extra 15 shillings
(75p) was awarded, but was postponed until February of the
following year. Then at the end of 1968 an increase of 17
shillings a week (85p) was awarded by the AWB, only to be once
more referred by the government to the Prices and Incomes
Board. The award was a 7.3 per cent increase, more than double
the government limit, and the government therefore tried to
freeze 7 shillings of it, much to the annoyance of the union. The
PIB, however, ruled that the full rise was justified as a special
exception.

Because of all this there was enough dissatisfaction with the
government at the union's 1969 Chester conference for Wilf to
successfully move withdrawal of support for the prices and
incomes policy. He argued that it had led to a cut in real wages
for members. General secretary Harold Collison opposed the
motion on behalf of the executive, on the grounds that a wages
free-for-all would put workers in less powerful unions at a
disadvantage. Wilf beat the leadership, however, winning his
motion by 64 votes to 54. As a result, at the 1970 Labour Party
conference the union voted for a TGWU motion to end incomes
restraint, and the government policy was defeated by a large
majority.

Wilf later recalled what had led up to this:

One of the rises awarded by the Agricultural Wages Board was
challenged by the Labour government and referred to the
Prices and Incomes Board. It was only a matter of a few bob a
week. The board's investigation did, however, prove beyond
doubt that farm workers got very minimal perks. People used
to say that farm workers don't have to worry about their
wages because they get free milk and free other things.

Farmers would say my boys are all right, I give them a turkey for Christmas. The investigation showed that only a very low percentage of their income came from perks. The annual wage negotiations were a bit of a charade. I wanted the union to take action and come out on strike, but the leadership did not want that. They did not mind members coming to London to protest outside the Ministry of Agriculture, but not much more. They had no clout really. I have been on loads of demonstrations when we took busloads of members from Norfolk and elsewhere to the negotiations. But the independent members on the wages board would always be on the side of the farmers and outvote the union members. Only once did they cause a ripple and then the chairman was replaced as punishment.

Wilf also spoke out against the executive at the 1969 conference, criticising it for delays in wage settlements and for not negotiating a high enough rate. His amendment was defeated, however, by 105 votes to 44. As he later recalled:

I was very critical of the leadership, which was not giving a strong enough lead. The increase in wages did not come up to the rise in the cost of living, and they were dabbling with bonus schemes and higher overtime and piecework rates. These, in my opinion, were the wrong target. They should have been campaigning for higher basic pay. The rest was peripheral. If you were on piecework you had to work like hell and not get much out of it, and bonuses were normally a fiddle. The leadership did not want an outright clash with the bosses on the question of wages.

The union was also losing strength, as members left the industry. But the leadership said that this did not matter, as they thought the shortage of farmworkers would enable them to command higher wages – and they did not have to recruit more members. That of course was a load of codswallop. As soon as the farmers got rid of the men they got more sophisticated machinery to take their place. But nothing was done by the union to stop people leaving. Some of the general secretaries seemed more interested in getting on to boards than giving rallying calls to the members.

There was some success in boosting members' earnings, however, and one of the factors was the increase in training, after the establishment of the Agricultural, Horticultural and Forestry Industrial Training Board in 1964. As chairman of the Norfolk Agricultural Training Board, Wilf supported efforts for improving training:

We fought for and got apprenticeships for farm workers. For three years they were trained off the farms at agricultural colleges two days a week. If they passed their exams they got a certificate and a premium on their wages. The government paid for it, but the curriculum was worked out by us in the industry and the employers and union worked well together on the boards. It was invaluable for training on new equipment. Before that, recruitment consisted of farmers trying out young lads at weekends or during holidays. The training scheme changed all that.

Training on new machinery was crucial, not least because agriculture had – and still has – the highest rate for deaths at work of all industries, but the union's safety campaigns and schemes tended to be resisted by the farmers on grounds of cost. (And recently the scheme for roving safety representatives has been rejected by the Health and Safety Executive – on cost grounds.) Safety was another issue on which Wilf campaigned:

> There was new machinery with hazards we had never before experienced. We fought for a long time to have a safety representative from the agricultural workers in each area, who would be entitled to look at the equipment on any farm – like in the building industry. But it never came, because of opposition from the farmers. They were quite happy to have inspectors come round as long as they gave them notice. One great victory we did achieve though was to get safety cabs fitted on tractors. The farmers even resisted that on the grounds of expense, but when it became law the number of accidents and injuries was greatly reduced.

The Tractor Cab Regulations, introduced in 1967, reduced the number of workers killed by overturned tractors from 25 a year to one or two.

Both Wilf and Christina were active in campaigning for equal pay in the 1960s. Christina's speech on the subject at the 1965 TUC conference in Brighton was reported in the *Daily Mirror*, with an accompanying photograph. She was reported as saying that women in industry were very disappointed that there had been no reference to equal pay in the Queen's Speech: 'Too many firms employ women as cheap labour ... I have always believed that when we had a Labour government we should have social justice. I call on this Congress to press for immediate legislation on this vital issue.'

Later Christina joined Wilf, who, in his role as secretary of the Eastern Counties Federation of Trades Councils, presented a petition of 1,200 signatures in support of equal pay to their MP in London. The campaign for equal pay was widely supported, and led to the Equal Pay Act, brought in by Minister of Employment Barbara Castle in 1968. (However, Castle was less popular the following year, when she published the *In Place of Strife* white paper, which proposed restraints on free collective bargaining, including proposals for compulsory strike ballots and cooling-off periods during which industrial action would be illegal.)

CPGB activities

Wilf was by now playing a national role in the Communist Party, where he made strenuous efforts to promote awareness of countryside issues. In 1961 he was pictured doing farm work on the front page of a pamphlet entitled 'Meet the Communists', which set out the party's plan for agriculture. 'While socialism implies the eventual public ownership of all land, the first step – taking over the large landed estates – would immediately improve conditions for thousands of tenants,' it stated. 'Increased agricultural production requires help to farmers, measures to bring more land into use, improved village amenities, and, above all, farm wages and conditions of work comparable with those in other skilled industries.'

He was also the district party secretary for East Anglia (on a voluntary unpaid basis) from 1960 to 1968, when the district was disbanded. For one meeting he travelled all the way to Clacton to give a talk – and only one person turned up. He had more success at other times, however, helping to form branches at Chelmsford, Colchester, Ipswich, Kings Lynn and Yarmouth.

A great friend of Wilf's in the East Anglian party district was the historian Leslie (A.L.) Morton. Morton was also on the district committee of the party and had bought a house in Willoughby Road, Ipswich, for the district offices. It had two rooms for offices on the ground floor, while the upstairs floor was rented out. Morton lived in Leiston, Suffolk, a village that had elected Communist councillors on a number of occasions, partly because of its connections with the nearby libertarian Summerhill School, run by A.S. Neill. Wilf had addressed the Leiston trades council as a speaker, and also spoken in the Leiston Post Office Square. He was very interested in Summerhill school and often visited it. Leslie Morton had taught there in the past, and his brother Max taught English and played hockey there. Max had three horse breeding farms, and let the party use them for youth camps and seminars. Those days were remembered by AEU engineering union member Daphne Oliver, also of Leiston, where she was chair of the local trades council (the first woman to hold such a post in the whole of England). 'While others mouthed the party line on the district committee, Wilf was not afraid to express a different view if it was based on his own experience,' she recalled.

In 1967 Wilf was elected to the national executive committee of the party, and he continued as a member of this committee for a further six years. Probably the most heated debate during these years was the discussion about the Soviet Union's invasion of Czechoslovakia in 1968. Though the party had supported the 1956 Soviet invasion of Hungary, the changing political tide meant that the invasion of Czechoslovakia provoked widespread debate – both within the British party and the international communist movement. Wilf supported the position finally adopted by the executive, which was to oppose the invasion: 'you couldn't have socialism without the local people themselves wanting it'. His argument was that the party's position was not hostile to the Soviet Union, but 'comradely critical'.

Generally, though, Wilf felt frustrated on the executive committee: 'They got on my wick somewhat by always setting up subcommittees rather than getting out and doing anything … I remember the general secretary John Gollan saying we must sell more *Morning Stars*. Sure enough they just set up a subcommittee rather than going out and selling them.'

Wilf had also noted an apparent lack of interest in the countryside on the executive committee, and all this meant that when, in 1973, the political committee (the highest party committee) did not put his name forward for continued membership of the EC, he decided against a challenge to their decision.

Union executive member

1969 was the year of a huge personal triumph for Wilf. On 24 June he received a letter from the union's general secretary Harold Collison (by now Lord Collison), informing him – one suspects somewhat grudgingly – that he had been elected on to the executive committee, representing Norfolk, by 4,767 votes to 2,837. At last! It had taken him seventeen years to achieve. He was the first and only communist ever to serve on the executive. In fact, the leadership's hostility to him was to wane fairly soon after his election. As he observed, 'they realised I was a fairly responsible character, and no obstacles were put in my way'.

Indeed, within three months he had been chosen to speak on behalf of the union at the Trades Union Congress in Portsmouth. As Wilf reached the rostrum to begin his speech, by chance the Labour leader and prime minister Harold Wilson mounted the stage behind him, and this prompted a loud round of applause. 'I thought the applause was for me,' said Wilf, 'and it greatly boosted my confidence as I had been rather nervous.' His spirited speech was in support of expanding agriculture, which, he argued, would save the cost of importing food. At that time Britain spent well over £750 million a year on imported food, much of which could have been produced at home. As Wilf pointed out, with the right government support output could be increased sufficiently to save £220 million a year within four years. However he also warned that such improvements could not be made without also improving the conditions of farm workers: 'The farm worker will respond to any call to increase production from our farms, but my union is convinced that the industry cannot face this issue with a labour force that is super-exploited. We cannot tolerate a situation where farm workers receive an average of about £7 a week less than the national average.' In conclusion he called on industrial workers to join with agricultural workers to bring pressure to bear on the government to pursue this import-saving programme. This time the applause really was for him, and the motion was passed with an overwhelming majority.

1. Note on comparative wages

In 1966 the legal minimum weekly pay for male agricultural workers was £10.80 (equivalent to £150.79 in 2008 prices). A Ministry of Labour publication for that year gave average weekly earnings of male agricultural manual workers as £13.62; for all male manual earnings outside agriculture it was £20.25. In 1967 the legal minimum weekly pay for male agricultural workers was £11.55 (equivalent to £157.12 in 2008 prices). In 1968 the legal minimum weekly pay for male agricultural workers was £12.40 (equivalent to £161.18 in 2008). The Department of Employment and Productivity's New Earnings Survey for that year gave median weekly earnings for full-time manual male workers as £15.90 in agriculture and horticulture, and in all industries and services as £22.40. Thanks to Lewis Emery at Labour Research Department for supplying this information.

9. The 1970s

Joan Maynard, the union's isolated left-wing vice-president, welcomed Wilf to the union executive with open arms, as a kindred spirit. Eight years younger than Wilf, she had been born and bred in the Thirsk area of rural North Yorkshire, and had spent her life battling with the establishment against injustice (including the labour movement establishment).

Wilf and Joan had first met in 1954 at the union's biennial conference in Cheltenham, when the nationalisation of land had been debated. One early disagreement, however, had been over the degree of nationalisation that should be proposed. Joan was in favour of calling for the nationalisation of all land, but Wilf favoured limiting the take-over to the large estates, which would then be divided into viable working farms run by co-operatives. Unlike Joan, he did not believe that they should call for smallholdings to be nationalised. He believed that it was important to find allies, to win the small farmers on to their side against the big farmers. This philosophy informed his approach to the different factions on the union's executive. He advised Joan to adopt a similar approach, in order to survive – but this did not suit her swashbuckling style.

Joan had been elected as vice-president of the union at the 1966 conference in Weston-super-Mare. Support for her candidature had derived largely from those who had participated in the widespread movement of 1965 against the Labour government's Rent Bill, which had failed to deliver on earlier promises to legislate against evictions of farm workers from tied cottages. Wilf and Joan had both criticised the union's executive for backing down on this issue. On being elected to the leadership – unlike many others in the past – Joan did not mellow her position. 'She came to the microphone and had a real go about the leadership, although she was on the platform,' recalled Wilf. 'It showed tremendous courage to do that.' She was almost powerless once on the executive, however; there was often nobody there who would even second her proposals – until Wilf was elected. Her eyes lit up when he attended his first meeting, and she told him how wonderful it was to have a friend at last, and how terrible it had been to be alone against thirteen other people 'out to get her'. However, Wilf had some tactical advice for her: 'Whilst I admire your courage, we must always remember that courage is not enough. We must at all times consider tactics and always try to avoid uniting our opponents. It would be a disaster to give the right wing the opportunity to remove you from office.'

Unfortunately, the right wing of the union did manage to achieve Joan's removal, at the 1972 union conference in Weymouth, when they completely abolished the post of vice-president. Their unconvincing claim was that this was in order to save money (a mere £400 a year), and had nothing to do with any antagonism towards Joan herself. Calls for a card vote were ignored, and after a show of hands it was ruled that the motion had been carried by 50 votes to 37. This was immediately challenged as a miscount, and Wilf demanded a recount. But this was rejected by the chair amid uproar (even though the rules stipulated that if a vote was disputed the president had to take another vote). Peter Medhurst (later the union's organiser based in Norwich) was one of many delegates who were convinced that the vote had been against abolishing the post: 'I saw the hands go up'. According to Wilf: 'As vice-president Joan went to different county conferences to speak on behalf of the union. She'd get her expenses to get there, probably overnight accommodation and some subsistence. But if the national officer went, he got his travel allowance, and he'd get his wages for the Saturday – he'd get double time for working on a Saturday and probably treble time for working on a Sunday. It was a terrific bill. So she was really saving money, but they used that as the excuse. They couldn't find another excuse. They didn't want her as vice-president as she was having far more influence than they wanted her to have.'

Joan bounced back however. She was elected as Labour MP for Sheffield Brightside two years later; and two years after that she succeeded in seeing through Parliament the Act that would finally prevent farm workers from being made homeless by eviction from their tied cottages.

The Tory government 1970–74

In 1970 there were two elections. One saw Wilf stand for the post of union president – in which he was beaten by 89 votes to 21. The other was the general election, which resulted in a victory for the Tories, and the installation of Edward Heath as prime minister.

Within a few months the new government introduced its first anti-union legislation, the Industrial Relations Bill. One of its measures was the setting up of a National Industrial Relations Court – which could punish unions but not employers. The court could impose legally binding agreements; and all solidarity or sympathetic action was outlawed. If unions did not register they could face unlimited fines for taking industrial action.

In March 1971 Wilf was part of the union's delegation to a special conference of the TUC to discuss resistance to the Act. He supported the proposal that unions should not register or co-operate with the legislation in any way – and this was adopted as a recommendation by the conference. However, five months later the right wing majority on the union executive decided to register, for financial reasons. But this was later reversed, at the union's 1972 conference, when Wilf's comrade Jack Dunman (editor of the *Country Standard*) moved a successful motion to deregister forthwith. (The NIRC was abolished by the Labour government in 1974.)

This resurgence of militancy was also evident during the 1972 national agricultural pay talks. Security for the talks that year was heightened because in the previous year some protesters had managed to enter the Ministry of Agriculture building and make their way to the room where the talks were taking place. They had slung a stinking dead chicken at the negotiators and shouted: 'Our wages smell like this does'. Police therefore restricted the number of people who could lobby the talks at the building entrance to 12, one of whom was Wilf. A big Rolls Royce turned up and Wilf decided that this was probably the chairman of the wages board. Accordingly the lobbyists started shouting at the figure who emerged from the car: 'How would you like to work in shit and mud for our wages?' After the dignitary had entered the building a policeman told them: 'Fat lot of good that did. That was the prime minister of Manila'.

A few minutes later a much more modest car arrived containing James Prior, the minister of agriculture and a Suffolk farmer, who had played football for Norwich City in his youth. For once this cut no ice with Wilf, though he was a keen Norwich fan. 'We started shouting again,' he said, 'and I got hold of the handle of the car door and opened it:

> And there he was sitting back in the car, wondering what the hell was going on. He had just given the farmers a £50 million fertiliser subsidy, so I shouted we want some of that £50 million. I was wearing a new set of false teeth and as I was shouting they shot out in his direction. I did a real Botham job in the slips and just managed to catch them before they landed on his trousers. He looked completely flummoxed. The rest of the boys killed themselves laughing as I tried to get my teeth back in as he went off.

The pay talks ended with the Agricultural Wages Board awarding a 20 per cent rise at the end of October, bringing the standard minimum rate to £19.50 a week. A few days later, however, this was overturned, when the Heath government imposed a pay freeze; the rise was delayed until the following April. Rumours abounded in the press that this freeze would lead to direct action, including strikes, and the watering down of milk at dairy farms by the workers. Wilf, as chair of the Eastern Counties Federation of Trades Councils, denied these reports, but did report that an overtime ban had been recommended.

This was a time of great industrial militancy, with many major battles being fought out between the government and employers and the labour movement. Not to be outdone by actions such as the famous occupation of the Upper Clyde Shipbuilders yard in Glasgow in 1971, Wilf became involved in a sit-in of his own. This was in Great Yarmouth at the Sextons shoe factory, which was scheduled for closure. Secret service MI5 files mentioning Wilf's role in this occupation are in existence, and have been seen by Norwich Labour MP Ian Gibson. Sadly, however, MI5 declined a request to provide more information on this, on the grounds that it was not covered by the Freedom of Information Act.

Campaigning against the common market

Another big issue during the years of the Tory government was Heath's determination to take Britain into the European Union – or Common Market as it was then called (and later the European Economic Community). This would have major implications for agriculture, not least because of the common agricultural policy. Wilf was in the forefront of the campaign within the union against joining the Common Market. However, many on the union executive supported entry, in the belief that it would lead to higher food prices to the farmers and higher wages to the farm workers. Wilf viewed this argument as folly and moved opposition to entry: and this was carried by just one vote. There was, however, a much larger majority against entry when it came to the delegates conference at Whitley Bay. This made the agricultural workers the first trade union in the country to oppose entry. But in the end MPs in parliament voted in favour of entry in 1971 – without the referendum on the issue that many had called for.

To prepare the way for fitting in with Europe's free market conditions, parliament then voted to abolish all government subsidies to British agriculture – which had guaranteed minimum prices and markets to the industry since the 1947 Agriculture Act. Through the provisions of this Act, the government made up any difference between the current market price for agricultural produce and the agreed guaranteed price. This had enabled a degree of planned production and hence allowed farms a degree of security.

As Wilf had predicted, entry into Europe did not lead to higher prices to farmers and higher wages to farm workers. Instead, it turned Britain into a dumping ground for the surpluses of European farmers at the expense of British agriculture, which consequently suffered more job cuts. The common market also used restrictions on supply to keep food prices up, and this led to the existence of subsidised 'butter mountains' and 'wine lakes' of unconsumed food and drink; and later there were 'set-aside' payments to farmers to pay them to stop producing food at all.

During this period Christina had become chair of Cromer and district trades council, and she too was involved in local opposition to the Common Market and the Industrial Relations Bill. And she was also in demand as a speaker on made-to-measure corsetry and other women's undergarments – because of her work as a fitter for the Spirella company that manufactured them. One such talk she gave, with the assistance of a live model, was to Holt Young Farmers' Club!

Local authority reorganisation

When the structure of local government was reorganised in 1974, Wilf thought it was time to stand down as a councillor, after his 28 years of service. 'By that time I had become very much involved in trade union activity and was away from home quite a lot,' he explained:

I felt a bit guilty that I was not carrying out my local work with the council. Also, the reorganisation meant that, instead of councillors being responsible for one village each, they now had about six. This meant I would never have been able to go to every parish council meeting and pass on resolutions to the council for what each village wanted, as I had done with Edgefield.

The reorganisation had been carried out following the findings of the Royal Commission on Local Government Report by Lord Redcliffe-Maud, which had recommended that more than one thousand local authorities should be abolished, to be replaced by a three-tier system under huge regional councils. These measures were passed into law in 1972, with local elections then being held in 1973, to produce 'shadow authorities' that would finally take over in 1974. The local councils at the bottom would henceforth have only limited and advisory powers. Wilf had expressed his opposition to these proposals in a *Morning Star* article in 1969, and he also expressed them in his county council election leaflet of 1973, just before the changes came in. His argument was that there was a danger that the disappearance of so many local councils would destroy democracy in local affairs, with decisions being taken without the knowledge of the local inhabitants. Wilf had always been an activist rooted in democratic local activity, and he was dismayed at this cavalier abolition of a whole tier of grassroots institutions.

The proposed changes were said to be in response to the huge increases in local council expenditure. But, as Wilf pointed out, this had been mainly due to the huge increases in interest charges that had been imposed on councils by the Town and Country Planning Act brought in by the Tories in 1959. As he had pointed out over a very long period of time, interest payments were draining local government of resources. His argument was that finance should be made available to councils for social building at low rates of interest, through a Public Works Loan Board; and he also believed that councils would be able to raise more funds through a local income tax rather than through the rating system, which was a regressive tax which fell more heavily on the poor than the rich (now replaced by council tax, which remains regressive). Yet neither of these potential remedies to the problem of local authority finance had been considered in the Maud report.

Wilf was also concerned that the increased time that would be needed to properly represent constituents in the new system would effectively exclude working-class people from standing. The report's 'very nice phrases' made 'no reference to the fact that large sections of the working class are unable to take on local council responsibilities through being unable to have two or possibly three days a week off from work.' At this time there were no allowances for attending council meetings and it was very difficult for most ordinary people to take time off from work to carry out such responsibilities. Wilf argued that it was 'high time that a person who enjoys the confidence of his fellow citizens should by right be able to attend council meetings.'

Labour government 1974–9

In 1974 the Labour Party returned to government. It very soon repealed the hated Industrial Relations Act and replaced it with the Employment Protection Act. However the issue of pay restraint remained on the agenda, this time being pursued through the 'Social Contract', which soon became a major political bone of contention. The idea was for a contract between the government and the TUC, whereby the unions would agree to moderate pay increases in exchange for promises of social justice measures, cutting unemployment and controlling prices. After the February election Labour could only form a minority government, and it therefore planned to call another election in the same year: it was hoped that the social contract would help Labour to win this.

The union's executive supported the social contract, provided that lower paid workers were given adequate protection against inflation – which in the event they were not.

Joan Maynard, who had been a Labour NEC member since 1972, and had now been returned as an MP, was opposed to the contract, however, calling for the restoration of full free collective bargaining; and Wilf shared her view. At the Norfolk county conference of the union he outlined his position:

> We are told we are all in the same boat under it. But five per cent of the population still owns 49.6 per cent of the nation's wealth. We are still two nations. Workers should not be taken in by propaganda saying that they are threatening the existence of a Labour government. Local and by-election results showed that it was the Tory policies of the Labour government which threatened its existence.

It was also in 1974 that Wilf dramatically drew attention to the health hazard of dust, which was responsible for the widespread incidence of chest diseases in both the agricultural and mining industries. In a speech at the TUC conference of that year he stated:

> The protection afforded to the agricultural worker does not begin to compare to that given to his colleagues of the factory

floor, despite the fact that the combine harvester is virtually a mobile factory, and the storage of grain gives rise to an obvious dust hazard. Yet there is no mandatory requirement for the fitting of dust extracting plant, or the provision of adequate masks.

He then produced a dust mask for display, pointing out that – far from giving adequate protection – it merely gave the wearer a false sense of security. Supported by the National Union of Mineworkers, his proposal that all chest diseases be classed as industrial diseases was overwhelmingly carried.

Joan Maynard was determined that the new government would finally bring an end to tied cottage evictions, and had insisted there was a pledge on this in both the 1974 Labour election manifestos. According to Joan, the only person to oppose this proposal was Jim Callaghan, who was himself a farmer. The campaign against evictions gathered increasing strength during 1974 and 1975, with a series of union lobbies of parliament. Some of the farm workers were at first hesitant in the corridors of power, especially since most of the MPs they intended to lobby were Tories (who were in the overwhelming majority in rural seats). Labour firebrand MP Denis Skinner, an ex-miner, was very supportive of their cause, however, and encouraged them to demand action from their MPs. This gave them the confidence to refuse to be fobbed off, and they succeeded in making their case forcefully.

As part of the campaign Wilf drew attention to the case of a young farm worker who, having been made redundant, was living with his wife and baby daughter in a shed, while their two other children slept in the car. They had no plumbing, having to fetch water from a nearby factory, and had to cook on a primus stove. Wilf had played a leading role in their resistance to

A Ken Sprague union poster against tied cottage evictions, on the front page of Landworker *in 1975*

eviction, which had led to a high court recommendation that the family be allowed to continue their tenancy. This had been ignored however.

Joan Maynard finally got the Rent Agriculture Act through parliament in 1976, and this meant that from 1977 no evictions could take place from tied cottages without alternative accommodation being provided. Wilf praised Joan for 'fighting like hell' to get this legislation through: although evictions could still take place, the process would now become much less vicious, and farmers would have to prove their need for the house in question under the Agricultural Dwelling House Act. If after this an eviction was still allowed, the local council would immediately be obliged to find a house for the evicted tenant. Wilf's one misgiving was that this would delay the housing of other people on the waiting list. (More recently, of course, councils have less housing to offer, having been forced by central government to sell off their stock.)

Campaigning in print

Wilf became the editor of *Country Standard* in 1974, from where he continued to campaign for justice for rural workers (filling up any spare time gained from having given up his seat on Erpingham council). The journal had started life as the *Country Worker* in 1935, and was published by the Communist Party to promote the interests of rural workers under the editorship of E.M. Elliott, who worked for the *Daily Worker* and lived in Ipswich. It had changed its name to the *Country Standard* in 1936, after which the editorship was taken on by Wogan Philipps (who later inherited the title of Lord Milford, becoming the first Communist in the House of Lords). Jack Dunman took over as editor in May 1946.

Jack was an Oxford graduate who had worked on a farm in the 1930s to help his health, and had then joined the union and taken up the farm workers' cause. He had built up a branch at Charlbury, which became the largest in Oxfordshire, thanks to his work cycling round to the homes of members and potential members. Later he became county secretary and then county chair of the union, as well as being a full-time Communist Party official. On one famous occasion in 1950 he roused local public opinion sufficiently to prevent the evictions of two families from tied cottages in the village of East Hendred. As part of his campaign he addressed a hundred people for half an hour in the evening next to a telephone box, which provided the only public lighting in the village. When Jack died in 1973, Ron O'Toole took over as temporary editor of the journal for a short while (assisted by Bob Wynn), before handing over to a small collective in Norfolk, headed by Wilf.

Wilf soon showed his creative talents by penning the following poem, published in the paper:

They root out the hedges and cut down the trees
They destroy all the flora and kill all the bees
They buy huge machines and sack lots of men
They plough up the scrubland and tear up the fen
On Calamity Farm.

They rear calves on wood slats and keep hens in wire cages
They pay the farmworker very low wages
They use toxic chemicals to increase the yields
Then destroy surplus produce as it's still in the fields
On Calamity Farm.

The 'Third World' cries out for some of our bread
The overnight count reveals masses of dead
Whilst the wealthy nations have much food to spare
It's the profits that hold up the process to share
On Calamity Farm.

They scream there's no money to pay the food bill
Yet millions are spent to maim and to kill
The white man must act before it's too late
Before the whole world is engulfed in white hate
On Calamity Farm.

The dawn is breaking to a beautiful scene
With the world's population well fed and serene
With children all singing and dancing around
With people all kissing the bountiful ground
On our farm.

Wilf also wrote a highly acclaimed Communist Party pamphlet, *Farming to feed Britain, a policy for farmers, farm workers and consumers*, which was published in 1976. (He was still convenor of the party's agricultural advisory committee, though he was no longer on the executive committee after 1973).

One major part of the argument was his criticism of the harmful effects on agriculture of Britain's membership of the European Common Market. Many of the problems that had been foreseen in the campaign against entry had now become evident:

> The scrapping in 1973 of the price support system to farmers in preparation for Britain's integration into the Common Market and the Common Agricultural Policy led directly and quickly into chaos and the crisis of the latter part of 1974 ... Livestock producers did not have the resources to keep their animals through the winter, and the whole future of livestock production was threatened.

Noting that the stated aim of the Common Market was to reduce the number of farms by two-thirds, he pointed out the need to expand food production: 375 million of the world's population were currently facing starvation. Furthermore, it was unwise to move to an increasing reliance on imported food – reversing a policy brought in during the second world war to produce as much food as possible within Britain. Wilf argued that the biggest obstacle to the expansion of home food production was the nature of British capitalism. The market for British exported manufactured goods was dependent on payments with food products from foreign countries:

British capitalism has consistently opposed efforts to expand agriculture, for fear that too much food produced in Britain would adversely affect its policy of expanding exports [of manufactured goods]. It was only during the periods of war that this policy was reversed. In 1938 Neville Chamberlain, the Tory prime minister, in a notorious speech said that he was not in favour of special efforts to encourage agriculture. 'It would ruin the Empire and foreign countries which are dependent on our markets and they would no longer be able to buy our manufactures from us.' This statement was made only a few months before the outbreak of the second world war.

It was only when the German navy started to play havoc with our food supply lines that the government of the day realised that Britain had to look to British agriculture to provide a far greater proportion of our food requirements. The arable acreage was at an all time low; a huge acreage of permanent grass was often little more than rough grazing. Ploughing up campaigns were launched, with subsidies from the government. A number of further regulations were introduced and measures were taken to increase food production from British farms. For some years after the war the world shortage of food and the economic dislocation guaranteed a market for all the food that could be produced.

In this situation the 1945 Labour government embodied the wartime regulations into the 1947 Agriculture Act, in which the principle of guaranteed prices and assured markets was fundamental. This security to agriculture resulted in a 50 per cent increase in production over the pre-war period. With the return of the Tory government in 1951 the traditional policies of restriction returned, and for all the old reasons. When a deputation from the Women's Institute went to the ministry to advocate encouragement of domestic food production and gardening they were answered by the parliamentary under-secretary, Mr Nugent, with this argument – 'we must import horticultural produce from western Europe to pay for Britain's manufactured goods, such as machines and textiles, and for this reason a campaign on the lines of the wartime Dig for Victory drive is not required.' Almost the same words as Chamberlain's.

Today, with the serious world food and energy problem and the dramatically changed position of Britain in the markets of the world, there must be a real drive to expand food production from our own soil. The measures which played such an important part in lifting agriculture to its present high standards must not be ignored.

The provisions in the 1947 Agriculture Act for an annual price review, informing farmers well in advance what crops were needed and what price they would receive, were very important. Governments have not used the Act as it was intended, because they have laid stress on the clause 'such part of the nation's food as in the national interest it is desirable to produce in the UK.' This escape clause can be used to eliminate guarantees altogether if a government wishes. Farmers were quite rightly critical of the way the Act was implemented.

As has been pointed out, British agriculture, based on a policy of planned expansion, has an important contribution to make to strengthening the national economy. With a big balance of payments deficit we cannot allow agriculture to stagnate. Our farmers and growers now produce two-thirds of our temperate food requirements. This figure could be and must be lifted much higher.

This acknowledgement of the need for domestic food production is something that has returned to the agenda with a vengeance in recent years. And Wilf was also ahead of his time in the concern he expressed, both in this pamphlet and elsewhere, about protecting the environment (and producing nutritious food) when new 'agribusiness methods' were introduced.

Farming to feed Britain called for the re-establishment of guaranteed prices and markets for food production, the nationalisation of 'a substantial part of the land', the establishment of co-operatives, and a reduction in the gap in wages between rural and urban workers: 'the fact that in the last decade 200,000 workers have left agriculture shows how poorly wages and conditions compare with those in other industries'. And it stated the belief that the fight for a prosperous and expanding agriculture was 'an integral part of the general struggle against the lowering of living standards of the people by monopoly capitalism'. As Wilf argued, the whole of the country's resources needed to be harnessed for the people's benefit, to 're-equip our industries, house our people, banish poverty and unemployment for ever, and raise living standards higher than anything we have ever known'. He ended on a rousing note: 'Only the vision of real social change will inspire enthusiasm for a great advance.'

Sadly, the premiership of Jim Callaghan (who had recently succeeded Harold Wilson as prime minister) in general inspired little enthusiasm for great social change.

The culmination of two careers

Perhaps the pinnacle of Wilf's contribution to the labour movement was to be elected in March 1979 as president of the European Federation of Agricultural Workers' Unions (EFA), representing two and a half million farm workers and 100,000 small farmers. Though he had to retire as president the following year, after a heart attack, he carried on serving the EFA for another six years, visiting Brussels about twice a week, which he found a tremendous experience:

> Its aim was to bring together farm workers and small farmers in Europe to lobby the ministers in Brussels in the same way as the employers through the NFU and CBI did. In Italy they had catholic unions, communist unions and socialist unions all disagreeing at home. But under the one roof of the EFA they tried to get a consensus. If you break down the bloody stupid barriers, they are all in harmony. I got them agreeing to things that at home they would have opposed like mad. I gave them a lead and emphasised we'd got to have unity all the time because we'd got powerful forces fighting against us. The main benefit was they all got to know each other, what their problems were, and discovered the problems were the same wherever they lived. It was a wonderful experience and I thoroughly enjoyed it. It was a harmony of workers and small farmers.
>
> I've always been an advocate of this, particularly with small working farmers who don't employ labour. They are also exploited by monopoly capitalism. Multinationals rob the farmer as much as the farmer robs the farm worker. The large farmer uses the plight of the small farmers to get more from the government in the interests of agriculture, and then gets the lion's share of the pickings.

Christina had her own moment of glory at the TUC conference at Blackpool in September 1979, though this was somewhat overshadowed by the recent return of Margaret Thatcher's Conservative government. She was awarded the women's gold badge for her contribution to the union movement. By this time she was the longest serving member on USDAW's executive council, having represented the eastern division since 1965. She had also chaired the union's conference, in the absence of the president Syd Tierney. And she had been secretary of the union's Cromer branch for 23 years, during which time its membership had increased from 32 to 200, and she had recruited another 800 members in other areas of Norfolk, in her role as vice-chair of the county's federation of branches, which she had held for fifteen years.

She had been a life long supporter of women's rights at work, and in 1975 had appeared on Anglia Television in a programme called *Time to Work*, which gave advice and encouragement to women on overcoming obstacles to paid employment. For many years she was the only woman on the union's executive, and had represented the TUC on the Women's National Commission.

The union journal *Dawn* carried a tribute, in which it reported that Christina had been a youth leader and a dancing teacher in her time and had also worked on international children's camps: 'In her nursing days, Christina was a member of NALGO for ten years, but she's been associated with USDAW and its fights for workers in parts of retailing and the laundry trade for so long that it seems hard to imagine her in any other trade union fold.'

Naturally Christina used the occasion of receiving the gold badge to get over some stirring political points:

When in 1945 a Labour government was elected with a large majority and a progressive policy, the trade union movement had high hopes of building a socialist society where the strong care for the weak and where the wealth of the nation would be more equitably shared. Where men and women would work together in equal partnership to remove the social evils of poverty, ignorance and exploitation from these islands. But we underestimated the power of the forces that intended to frustrate our activities and today we have a Tory government in power which is hell bent on dismantling the gains which the trade union movement has so strongly advocated and defended. We must not allow this to happen; we must go on the offensive to prevent this wanton destruction of our education, health and social services. Their policy will have disastrous effects on our children, the elderly, sick and the poor in our society.

Our scientists and engineers have produced for us the means of increasing the productivity of labour a thousand fold. We welcome these new achievements of advanced technology, but we must make sure new techniques do not create a small elite of highly skilled operators at work with a mass of our people stagnating and frustrated in the dole queues. We cannot accept this waste of human energy, which creates such misery and hardship.

In any economic crisis it is the women and coloured workers who suffer the worst effects of unemployment. I would appeal to any woman in work and not yet a member of her appropriate trade union to join immediately for she is going to need the protection of the organised movement. If all workers unite we can halt this government and take for all time that socialist road which so many workers have worked for, and yes, died for.

Christina went on to thank Wilf for his help and consideration over the years: 'for it was he who first persuaded me to read and become involved in the movement'.

Later it was Will's turn to take the rostrum, to move a

resolution that membership of the EEC (which the Common Market had by now become) be reconsidered. He argued that the Common Agricultural Policy was harming the British economy and its working people, and that the country's contribution to the community budget was far too high. As he pointed out, a large proportion of this budget was 'absurdly spent on dumping or storing surpluses'. He called on the government 'to negotiate an end to the present imbalances in levies, intervention payments and stockpiling'. And he succeeded in winning a unanimous vote in favour of the resolution.

10. Retirement and continuing activism

In 1980 the agricultural workers' union conference was due to be held in Great Yarmouth, but after it was discovered that the fascistic National Front was also holding its conference there it was decided to boycott the venue. At short notice, Cromer pier was selected as the new venue, and this meant that a huge amount of advance organising was required, the main burden of which fell on Wilf's shoulders (he continued this organisational work during the conference itself, behind the scenes in the dressing room of comedians Hinge and Brackett, who were appearing on the pier in the evenings). Shortly after this he had a heart attack. For a brief period he was actually clinically dead, but fortunately he was resuscitated and placed in intensive care.

Union officials were under strict instructions not to disturb him under any circumstances. But it took more than a heart attack to stop Wilf from campaigning. As Chris Kaufman, then the assistant editor of *Landworker*, recalls:

> Then I got a phone call from him, still in intensive care, asking me what had been done to progress his resolutions on organic phosphates and the pay claim from the conference. He was supposed to be at death's door but he was already back in harness and determined to overcome all obstacles. Then he told me that when he had been clinically dead he had felt an out of body experience and that he had seen God. He was winding us up with his own distinctive brand of humour. But the nurse was genuinely shocked when he revealed to her that God was a black woman.

The Cromer conference had adopted a number of important decisions, one of which was a reassertion of the union's policy of land nationalisation. In spite of his poor health Wilf was prominent in the campaign to promote the idea. 'The campaign attracted a huge amount of publicity and there were a lot of attacks on the policy,' recalled Francis Beckett, at that time the editor of *Landworker*. 'We got lots of requests for television and radio interviews and Wilf insisted on coming up to London for them, despite suffering from crippling back pains. He went from place to place doing great interviews against hostile questioning and getting our case over cogently. It was like watching the master at work.' Beckett described Wilf as an 'electrifying speaker'.

Wilf had laid out an eloquent case for land nationalisation in an earlier speech at the TUC. He argued that the state should become the farmers' landlord, so that farmers could be guaranteed security of tenure. It was simply a question of taking back common land that had been stolen from the people by the ancestors of today's large landowners: 'From history we know that men – hungry men who stole a sheep from the common – found themselves on the scaffold, while men who stole the commons from the sheep found themselves sitting in the House of Lords.'

Another crucial decision taken at the Cromer conference was to resist pressure to merge with a bigger union – for example with the Transport & General Workers Union – in order to ease growing financial problems. (The vote against was 69 votes to 39.) Wilf was strongly opposed to amalgamation. He was particularly concerned to keep the close personal contact the union had with its members, which he thought would be lost in an amalgamation:

> Every farm worker knew who their area representative was as we had a very close sort of village democracy. That sort of village culture was going to disappear with computerised membership systems and deduction of union dues direct from wages. We knew the dockers and other TGWU members, who were very powerful and marvellous characters, but I felt they would overpower the farm workers when they went to conferences, and the voice of the farm worker, which was the voice of rural trades unionism, would disappear.

But as the union finances reached crisis point, a recalled conference was held in November of the same year to reconsider the decision. This time the vote was narrowly for a merger, by 47 votes to 39. As Wilf put it: 'The case was made that if we did not merge now we would completely run out of money and would have to go creeping to other unions to accept us under any conditions. And we could not refute it really'.

Things were not made easier by a six-week strike in 1982 by

1200 members at the Bernard Matthews' Norfolk turkey factories. This cost thousands of pounds each week in strike pay, which the union did not have the funds for. Peter Medhurst recalled that Wilf had played an important role in this strike:

> He stiffened up the union executive to keep supporting the strike, organised welfare service to support the strikers, raised money for their hardship fund, and kept morale up. If Wilf had not been there it would have been more difficult for the people to last it out. The most important thing was to get everybody reinstated, which is why it lasted so long. Wilf worked very well with the convenor, A J Rudd, whom he had identified as someone who could lead.

Wilf had also been very much involved in another strike at that time, at Middlebrook Mushrooms in Cromer. But the cost of these strikes was crippling for the union, and all this made seeking a merger more urgent.

In the TGWU

The union now had to decide who to approach for amalgamation. USDAW, the shopworkers union, and the GMWU (general and municipal workers) were both considered, but in the end it was the TGWU that was approached. Wilf was in favour of this choice:

> I wanted to go into the TGWU because they had got lorry drivers visiting farms and this could be used to build up a relationship. And politically they were more in line with my own thinking. I didn't want to lose the voice of the rural worker, and the TGWU agreed that we should have our own

autonomous trade group with our own national secretary and executive committee. That rather appealed to me. And they also said they would keep publishing the union journal, *Landworker*, which I thought was vital. It was often the only contact the farm workers had with the union. I managed to persuade the negotiating team, by a small margin, that we ought to go in with the T&G.

This recommendation was approved in a ballot of the membership in 1981, and the merger was completed in 1982.

Having been excluded from union schools thirty years earlier, Wilf was by now one of the tutors. At one session, at a school at Beatrice Webb House in Dorking in 1982, during the dark days of the Thatcher government, he took the opportunity to urge the students not to be pessimistic but to build up the struggle. He recalled how Paul Robeson had changed the words of Old Man River from 'tired of living but scared of dying' to 'I must keep fighting until I'm dying'. One of the students took this too literally in the pub that evening: after an inebriated political argument with one of the locals he pole-axed his adversary with a garden gnome. 'The next day all our car tyres had been slashed,' recalled Chris Kaufman. Many of the students from Norfolk on that course became known as Wilf's 'Young Lions' (a sort of youth section of the union). They included Mike Ward, Dave Butt and Alan Lundie.

Wilf, by now a union elder statesman, was elected by the trade group of the TGWU which the union had now become to represent it on the full TGWU general executive council … by just one vote. The crucial vote came from a young member attending his first meeting of the trade group – a Welsh forestry worker called Ivan Monckton:

I arrived a bit late and there was just one seat left, next to Wilf, so I took it, and drank the cup of tea on the table. Wilf said you have just drunk my tea. There was then a heated debate about whether Wilf was eligible to stand for the TGWU executive and it was ruled he was. But he was so vehemently attacked by the right wing and responded so calmly and rationally that I voted for him because of his style.

Ivan went on to become the current trade group's representative on the TGWU (which is now part of Unite).

Unemployment rose dramatically during the early years of the Thatcher government, reaching 3 million by 1982. In 1981 Wilf, by now chairman of Norfolk Manpower Services Commission, was involved in setting up a centre for unemployed workers in Cromer. At its opening he announced: 'This is not a soup kitchen and we are not here to knit socks for the unemployed'. Cost price soup was available, however, to help supplement a diet that tended to deteriorate during long periods of unemployment. The main aim was to break down the 'complete sense of isolation' felt by the unemployed, especially in rural areas. One of its first projects was to collect toys for the children of people out of work. When the People's March for Jobs against unemployment was organised by the TUC in 1983, Wilf drove his camper van to act as a mobile hospital for the marchers. Christina was on board to treat sore feet and legs. 'A Trotskyist marcher was suffering with bad feet, but said he was not letting a "Stalinist" touch him,' recalled Mike Ward. 'Eventually the pain got the better of him and he swallowed his principles to allow Christina to treat him.'

After the march the TUC still had hundreds of unsold T-shirts advertising it. Wilf managed to blag them off the TUC, and went on to sell them for £1 each at Tolpuddle and other festivals to raise money for the *Country Standard*. Mike recalled that when a Russian delegation was visiting Cambridge they presented them with some of the T-shirts, to help expose the unemployment position, just after the mayor had made a speech: 'The local paper said we had compromised the office of mayor with this stunt, which was not our intention – but it was good publicity all the same.'

In 1984 Wilf, aged 70, was on the picket lines at Ipswich docks and Colchester in support of the national miners' strike. But he had to retire from the TGWU general executive, because of his age. The chair of the executive, Hull docker Walter Greendale, paid a glowing tribute to him:

> Wilf Page has done a magnificent job for farm and allied industry workers as their first representative on the T&G executive. It was no easy task to convey the farm workers' desire to maintain their treasured independence based on a proud history, whilst seeking to build alliances with their new-found trade group colleagues in the larger union. Wilf has managed it, though, with a dignified and statesmanlike forcefulness which springs from his wide knowledge and long history of struggle within the trade group and labour movement. He has won the respect of all the other regional and trade group representatives on the executive and, speaking personally, I have reason to appreciate Wilf's vast knowledge, experience and comradeship on a trade union delegation to the Soviet Union.

A letter in the TGWU *Record*, the journal of the whole union, praised Wilf's 'tremendous role in encouraging people into the movement, developing their political understanding and class consciousness, and supporting them in all their struggles'.

It concluded:

> Two of his qualities stand out. His willingness to work in an open way with others in helping them with any problems they wanted resolving (anyone who has spent an evening in his house will know all about the number of times the phone rings by someone seeking his help), and his kindness and understanding towards those bitterly opposed to his politics.

Wilf now became chair of the trade group in the union's largest region, which covered the whole of East Anglia and the South East. He retired as chair of Norfolk County Association of Trades Councils, however, and to mark his years of service he was presented by Norwich MP Ian Gibson with a Tolpuddle Martyrs platter, commemorating the 150th anniversary of their trial and transportation in 1834.

This was particularly fitting since Wilf had been a regular attender of the rally in Tolpuddle in July of each year that celebrates the memory of these pioneers of the trade union movement. Ian Gibson, who had once stood as a candidate in a local election with Wilf's son John, praised Wilf's dedication, particularly in all the cycling around Norfolk he had undertaken for the movement: 'That was a real commitment, and it was done to keep trade unionism alive and kicking in this county'.

Campaigning in East Anglia

Unable to stay idle for long, Wilf became involved in the resurrection of the Burston Strike School rallies. Originally these rallies had been held to raise money for the school that was run by Kitty and Tom Higdon from 1914 to 1939 (as described in the opening chapter). Wilf decided that the story should live on, and he therefore organised a rally and march in 1984, which has now become an annual event on the first Sunday of every September. Helping him to get the rally going again was his old comrade, Tom Potter, who was the brother of Violet, the pupil who had led the original strike at 13 years of age. Tom was born in 1910 and attended the Higdons' new school. He had lived in Burston all his life and, being both a Communist Party member and a local councillor, he was a natural ally of Wilf's; they were firm friends. Sadly, Tom died at the age of 75 just after the second annual rally.

The rallies have gone on to attract some of the top figures in the labour movement, who have used the occasion to tackle head-on some of the hot political issues of the day. This, combined with music and other entertainments, have made it an event of continuing popularity. Billy Bragg (whom Wilf had gone to Glastonbury to see in 1995, as we will see later) performed at the 2007 Burston rally and drew a record crowd.

During these years there was a massive growth in the peace movement, as the Thatcher government agreed to allow American cruise missiles carrying nuclear warheads to be based in Britain. The Snowball Campaign of direct action against American air force nuclear bases in Norfolk started in October 1984, after mass marches, letters and petitions had been ignored. The campaign aimed to get Britain to vote at the United Nations for multilateral nuclear disarmament, regardless of how the Americans voted, to publicly encourage America to freeze nuclear weapon growth; and to persuade the government to abandon Trident, return cruise missiles, and publicly reject American chemical weapon storage proposals.

As part of the campaign in Norfolk, three women cut single strands from the wire perimeter fence at the Sculthorpe air base, and then gave themselves up at the local police station. On appearing before Fakenham magistrates court, two of them were fined £160 each for criminal damage, while the third, Angela Zelter, who lived near Cromer at East Runton, was remanded and eventually imprisoned for breach of conditions from a previous obstruction charge at Greenham Common (one of the two proposed bases for the cruise missiles). The idea of the Snowball Campaign was that the number of protesters cutting the wire fence would treble each time until the authorities were unable to cope. The campaign lasted for three years, during which time 2,796 people were arrested for cutting wires at 42 military bases.

On Sunday 22 September 1985 Wilf joined in at Sculthorpe, when the target number was up to 243, in the full glare of television cameras. His diary entry for that day reads: '1PM

CUTTING FENCE'. He was arrested with other protesters and brought to Fakenham court, where he was fined £60 and ordered to pay £24.20 compensation and costs within 84 days. He told the court:

I cut the wire and plead not guilty to the charge of criminal damage. I joined Canon Collins and Bertrand Russell and their colleagues in the early 1950s campaigning against Blue Streak and other missiles as these were weapons of indiscriminate destruction of civilian population and property. We were told in those days that the Soviet Union was poised in Eastern Europe about to pounce on our country – therefore we had to have these weapons. It seems ludicrous to suggest that the Soviet high command has been poised for 30 years or more, patiently waiting for us to perfect a bomb that would destroy all life on this planet before pouncing on our country.

As a lad I was taught that David, in slaying the Philistine giant, did not commit a criminal offence. A nuclear bomb exploding by accident or other means at Mildenhall, Lakenheath or Sculthorpe, would result in my house at Overstrand disintegrating with the intense heat. This bomb reduces the Philistine Goliath to a mere child's firecracker. My colleagues and I are endeavouring to slay this giant, not with a sling, but an 18p hacksaw blade. I make reference to my house in Overstrand, but it is not in self interest that I cut the wire, but in the interests of everybody inside this court and outside.

I, like thousands of other Norfolk people, would much rather spend my time worrying about whether Norwich City will be playing First Division football next year. But how can we, any of us, live with devices in our midst that would bring horror, destruction and death that we cannot imagine, even in our worst nightmares? During the past 30 years I now have five other reasons for taking this action – they are my five grandchildren. [These were Carol's daughter Anna-Marie [Johnson], and John's children Jim, Ruth, Gaila, and Ross.] They must not be murdered by nuclear fall-out.

There is a glimmer of hope arising on the horizon that fortifies us in our efforts towards a successful conclusion. We must be successful.

Wilf also pointed out that 'criminal damage' seemed a ridiculous charge compared to the mass destruction that was being planned within the fences of the air base, and it would be more appropriate to charge the Conservative prime minister Margaret Thatcher under the Genocide Act for allowing it (a later attempt to do just this at Cromer magistrates court was rejected on grounds of 'frivolity').

Wilf refused to pay the fine and was expecting to be jailed when appearing at Fakenham court in December, after the time limit had expired. But it was paid anonymously on his behalf at the last minute, and so no action was taken against him (according to Peter Kentfield the fine was paid by Peter Melchett). Mike Ward, a fellow protester, was charged on the same day. He recalled that when they were in the dock the clerk of the court addressed the gallery, and, bearing in mind previous protests, stated that if anybody had it in their mind to start singing they should leave now: 'So Angela Zelter started to leave the dock, and the clerk immediately said: "Not you." Then she told him she had it in her mind to sing, which brought laughs all round.' (Later Angela made headlines again by helping cause a million pounds' worth of damage to a Hawk jet to prevent it being used for genocide in East Timor, and breaking into Faslane naval base and throwing nuclear weapons equipment overboard.)

Another campaigner in the dock with Wilf at Fakenham was
Lord Peter Melchett, who had been a Labour government
minister in the 1970s, was later executive director of
Greenpeace, and is now head of the Soil Association:

> I remember Wilf as a tall and authoritative, but very friendly
> figure, with a firm handshake. He was part of the vibrant
> force for social change of those days. You could rely on him
> for personal commitment, solidarity and support.

He and Wilf were immortalised in 'Snowball, a Modern Folk
Ballad', which was written by Barbara Smith to the tune of
Riddle-me-ree. It contains a small inaccuracy, to the effect that
Wilf pleaded guilty, but went:

> I ask you a riddle
> a riddle-me-ree
> If you can't explain it
> say Fiddle-de-dee.
>
> A communist and an English Lord
> seem a random enough selection
> yet I put a snowball between the two
> and ask you to spot the connection.
>
> An English Lord and a Communist
> went snowballing together;
> yet strange to tell and strange to hear
> it wasn't snowy weather.
>
> The fence was wide, the fence was high.
> Wire-cutters in their hand
> the English Lord and the Communist
> set out to reclaim the land.

Then up came a man in blue,
he was both stern and large;
'And what is going on here?' says he
'I'll have to put you on a charge.'

...

And when the two were brought to Court
the Magistrate was floored;
before him was a Communist
together with an English Lord.

Their offence was uncontested
and 'guilty' was their plea;
the Magistrate weighed the evidence
'You'll both pay fines' said he.

For 'It could only happen in England' they said
'Whoever would have so guessed
that an English Lord and a Communist
would join in a common protest?'

...

11. Pensioners' activist

The Transport & General Workers' Union gold medal was awarded to Wilf for his outstanding service to the union in 1986, presented to him by general secretary Ron Todd at a rally in North Walsham.

Later in the year, Wilf read the lesson at the Harvest Thanksgiving service in Norwich Cathedral, representing the union. As a novel way of representing the contribution of farm workers he took a tractor to the cathedral and drove it up the aisle. Explaining his views on religion to Rev Canon Colin Beswick, who conducted the service, Wilf reiterated his belief: 'The Bible says love thy neighbour as thyself, and the Union says an injury to one is an injury to all'. He acknowledged the principles, but not the spirituality of Christianity, and on one occasion recalled a seminar he had attended with Reverend Ron O'Toole (a marxist who had a brief spell as *Country Standard* editor). At the end, the clergyman said: 'You know, Wilfred, I shall never convince you about the Immaculate Conception, or life after death, but that long period in between – haven't we a lot in common!'

Wilf was also evidently perceived as having much in common with the Independent Order of Foresters, a fraternal benefit society: he was formally invited to join its Norwich branch in June 1988. Dating back to the time of Robin Hood, the order was formed for 'mutual aid and protection' and stood for 'liberty, benevolence, and concorde'. Its main principle was that 'united we may hold back adversity, which alone would overwhelm us'. This would certainly have fitted in with Wilf's trade union and socialist principles, but he did not take up the invitation. The fact that he was invited, however, is an illustration of Wilf's standing in the community.

In 1988 Wilf and Christina moved into a fisherman's cottage, Rose Cottage, at 1 The Londs, in Overstrand – which backed on to their old house. But retirement and inactivity did not suit Wilf, and he soon formed a retired members' association branch of the union in Norwich. 'It was a very good branch,' he said, 'but we had no real clout, so I suggested we formed a wider pensioners' organisation.' The result was the Norfolk & Norwich Pensioners' Association, which was set up in 1989 by Wilf and just nine others at a meeting in Norwich city hall. Within three months it had grown to 4000 members, in 20 different branches, under Wilf's chairmanship. 'We were amazed at the response,' he said. (Christina had by now been elected to the TUC Pensioners Committee.) The Norfolk & Norwich Pensioners' Association affiliated to Age Concern, but Wilf made it clear they were working in a different field: 'our aim was to fight for higher pensions'.

Support had grown so much that in July 1991 they were able to hire the Carrow Road football stadium of Norwich City for a rally, which was broadcast on Radio Norfolk. Wilf told the crowd that pensioners had won the right for a better deal. The present generation of pensioners had left school in the 1920s and 1930s, only to be confronted by mass unemployment and widespread poverty:

> When the government was urged to create employment by building badly needed schools, hospitals and roads they replied there was nothing they could do as they had no money. Yet Britain was one of the most wealthy nations in the world. Indeed it owned large sectors of the globe and exploited the mineral wealth and the people of the colonies in the interest of British big business. Labour camps were set up in the forests of Thetford, with young men sent there to undergo a harsh regime of work. Young farm workers were put to work breaking stones by the side of the roads to earn just enough to keep themselves alive.
>
> In September 1939 a transformation took place. This young generation suddenly became national heroes, prepared to destroy Hitler's war machine. New suits, new boots and underclothing were given to them, and railway warrants were issued like confetti for millions of miles of free public transport. Politicians changed their tune. All support had to be given to rid Europe of Nazism. There was no talk about where the money was to come from. Millions of pounds were poured into the war effort. Nobody asked can we afford it, there was no talk about economic crisis.

Sixty years later, this generation was now being told again there was not enough money for a decent pension. Wilf called for an immediate commitment to a pension equal to half the average gross earnings of workers. And he also argued that substantial

Wilf in later years
© *John Midgley*

reductions in fares should be granted to pensioners on all public transport nationally, and full community and social services should be made available to all who needed them.

It was small wonder that Norfolk & Norwich Pensioners' Association won the campaigning Age Resource Award at London's Royal Festival Hall in December 1991.

The end of the CPGB

This was also the year that, after 71 years, the Communist Party of Great Britain came to an end, with a new successor organisation, Democratic Left, being set up. This was a time when the Soviet system was crumbling, and many blamed its system of 'democratic centralism' for discouraging criticism of the status quo, and slowing down adaptation to changing circumstances. Those in favour of disbanding the Communist Party and setting up the new organisation believed that tight centralism (and accepting 'the party line' without question) should be replaced by a looser organisation, which would encourage debate both before and after decisions had been made. When the matter had to be thrashed out at the party's 43rd and last congress, at the TUC headquarters in London in November, many assumed that Wilf, aged 78, would be against the change.

Francis Beckett (in his history of the Communist Party, listed in the bibiography) described Wilf as 'tall, erect, dignified ... a widely read "worker intellectual" ... a great orator of the old open air school with a voice that sounded as though he gargled with granite.' According to Beckett, Wilf's political history suggested that he might well be a powerful voice against change – and, indeed, at first his speech sounded like that of a man from another age. Wilf told the delegates: 'The heroic struggles of the Soviet people during the war, and the important role they played in destroying the Nazi war machine, convinced us that the USSR would be an important element in building post-war society'. But then he surprised his audience: 'When Russian tanks rolled into Prague [in 1968] the whole underlying [Soviet] system was seen to be full of contradictions. Our younger comrades are not conditioned by our experiences ... We older comrades must shed our nostalgia, including the name of the organisation, and offer support and encouragement to these comrades ...'

The vote was 135 to 72 in favour of disbanding the old party.

Wilf confided afterwards that he had met too many 'old comrades clinging like hell to what they loved' – because it was hard 'to give your life to something and find out you have been wrong'. But he was never a man to avoid facing up to reality.

Wilf had been stunned when, in 1956, Nikita Khrushchev had spoken out about Stalin's regime (to which he was now the successor), and had outlined what had been perpetrated in the name of communism, including the liquidation of opponents, and the use of central administrative control to undermine democratic input in decision-making. 'I can't tell you what it was like, when Khrushchev made that speech,' he said:

> There were ten of us meeting in Ipswich, all steel hardened communists who had fought like hell and were really tough politically. We were almost in tears, some were in tears. To think the whole edifice we saw was crumbling and was a load of codswallop, and those ridiculing us at the time had been right, and we had been wrong.

Wilf was also dismayed as evidence of personal corruption by communist leaders in eastern Europe emerged after their downfall. Asked by the *Eastern Daily Press* what he thought of the excesses of Nicolae Ceausescu (the Romanian leader from 1965, who was shot in 1989 for crimes against the state, including genocide) he replied: 'I suppose I was naive. I didn't imagine people would do this in the name of communism or socialism'. Wilf had met Erich Honecker, the leader of the German Democratic Republic from 1971 to 1989, but had not for one moment realised that he was capable of crimes such as stowing away money in Swiss banks. As he commented: 'That's criminal enough, but he'll never be tried for the real crime, and that's bastardising communism.' Wilf had never had much time for Soviet leader Leonid Breshnev, however: 'I met [him] in East

Berlin, and he was a nasty humbug. You could imagine all sorts of things with him.'

As a scientific socialist, Wilf knew that it was better to objectively confront what had gone wrong, and learn from the experience, rather than to ignore unwelcome facts and rely on faith in a system (or those running it):

As time has gone on I have realised that communists have got to start thinking for themselves, working out things, not rely on other people, not accept anything without question. We did in those days. We accepted atrocities, the shooting of the Russian soldiers at the beginning of the war. Now we realise those boys were right and the hierarchy were fearful of them, and that was why they got rid of them.

So I think my Marxism has been enriched as a result of the downfall of the Soviet Union. I still think of myself, as I have done since the war, as a Marxist. I believe that the Marxist philosophy is going to ultimately emerge. It is not a dogma, it is an analysis of society and the forces within that society that make it advance, and an understanding of the reactionary force within society as well as the positive forces.

It also recognises that the only way reactionary forces are going to be overcome is by the workers themselves having a democratic say in the kind of society we have. Our present society is not a democratic society, it is a petty bourgeois democracy really. There is no democracy between Bernard Matthews and the workers in his factory. He has got far more power than they have got. That applies to all in our society. The press is owned by these people. They determine what people should think. This has all got to change and it is a tremendous job.

I'm optimistic. I think people are beginning to think for

themselves and create new ideas and new structures. The old militarist structure has got to disappear and new ones have to emerge from grassroots experience of life.

While he supported the ending of centralised militaristic structures, Wilf still thought there was a need for 'a disciplined Party based on Marxism' to explore the new way forward. And the Democratic Left, which he joined, did not fully live up to that.

His daughter Carol described his approach:

He thought the Communist Party was no longer effective as an organisation, and its links with the Soviet Union were impossible to overcome. Another title for the party, he thought, might enable the transformation to allow another step forward in the working-class struggle. Although he realised mistakes had been made and there had to be reform, he wanted to salvage what had worked, and question the things that had gone wrong, such as keeping power at the centre and undemocratic practices. But the political edge and the reality of the power struggle was always important for him.

As the Democratic Left became softer he had more problems with it. But he thought there was nothing better on offer and he understood that politics was an uphill struggle that had to be viewed in the very long term. It was just another phase in the gradual process to a better solution. Even if Democratic Left was not as strong as he wanted, he thought it was getting people thinking and moving in a helpful direction. So he still sold the Democratic Left paper [New Times] in his wheelchair in Cromer and carried on reading the Morning Star.

I asked him if he was bitter about giving up his whole life to the movement when the Soviet Union collapsed. He said:

'How can I be? It is just part of the process of change.' When I thought he would be despondent he was still positive, dynamic, and motivating others right up to the day he died.

As the pensioners' movement grew, a National Pensioners' Convention was formed and Wilf became its first vice-president. He also helped found a quarterly paper, the *Anglian Pensioner*, which had a wide circulation. As well as being on its management board, he contributed to it regularly and sold it in the streets. But after developing arthritis he retired from the movement in 1995, with a final plea, through the columns of the *Eastern Daily Press*, to the newly elected Labour Party leader Tony Blair to restore the link between pensions and the average earnings of workers. As he argued, Mrs Thatcher had removed the link in 1980 'by the stroke of a pen', and it was costing pensioners £17 a week. A future Labour government could correct this injustice 'also by the stroke of a pen'. Sadly that message went unheeded. In recognition of his work for the pensioners' movement Wilf was awarded the TGWU brass statuette in 1995 by Jack Jones, president of the union's retired members' association and the retired general secretary of the union.

In June 1995 Wilf achieved a reputation as 'the oldest hippy in town'. One of his grandsons had suggested that the Glastonbury pop festival would be a good event at which to sell the *Country Standard*. Fast approaching his 83rd birthday and needing a walking stick, Wilf gamely rose to the challenge. 'We were up to our eyes in mud', recalled Mike Ward, who accompanied him. 'Sadly we did not sell any *Country Standards*, as most of the audience were more interested in smoking dope':

We found Wilf's grandson who took us to see Billy Bragg. But as we were crossing a narrow bridge over a dyke, Wilf slipped off the edge and ended up in a ditch. Unperturbed, and caked in mud, he got up and went to see Billy Bragg. My wife said he was the oldest hippy on the site.

In 1996 Wilf moved into Halsey House, the British Legion home for ex-servicemen, in Norwich Road, Cromer. Built in 1946 to house 59 old or incapacitated residents in dormitories, it had been completely updated in 1984 to provide individual rooms for 64 people, having been awarded £1.25 million from the poppy appeal fund. Wilf

immediately formed a Musical Appreciation Society at the home, playing a mixture of popular standard records alongside his collection of more political songs by singers such as Paul Robeson. His love and rapport with birds was also recognised when he was made relief bird feeder for the home's aviary.

He made friends with a very conservative resident, who had been a major in the army. When the major heard Wilf had been in the RAF he teased him for being a 'bloody brylcreme boy', and Wilf sniped back at the army 'square bashers' in return. After Wilf had read his *Morning Star* and the major had read his *Daily Telegraph* they used to swap newspapers and hold heated political discussions. 'Although they had completely different political views they respected each other and had a great interaction,' said Carol.

Wilf was surprised one day to be visited by the local chaplain, none other than Reverend Ron O'Toole, whom he had first met in the Communist Party in the 1970s. Ron had been a farm worker on a Dominican friary farm and had set up a branch of the union there. Then he had met James Klugmann, through the Christian Marxist dialogue, and had joined the party. He later worked for Progressive Tours, where he often came into contact with Wilf, and was ordained in 1979. 'When I met Wilf again in the home he was still full of revolutionary ideas,' said Ron. 'He was a cut above the rest, full of integrity and genuineness. A friendly and humorous man, who never resorted to tub thumping, he was open and had a true generosity of spirit.'

In the same year, 1996, Wilf appeared on television, reminiscing about his early days, including the school strike he had led at the age of ten. He was in two of the series *A Man's World*, which were broadcast on BBC2 on 6 and 13 March.

In September, after his health had deteriorated further, he was presented with an electric wheelchair from local farm workers in the union. Thanking them, he said: 'Walking isn't too easy now, and it is wonderful to have a chair to bring me a whole new lease of life.' Then he promised: 'I'll never give up campaigning.' True to his word, he remained chairman of the union's Trunch branch for the remainder of his life. But he was finding it difficult to keep publishing the *Country Standard*. So in 1997 he and the collective agreed to incorporate it into *Greensocs*, the journal of the Green Socialist Network.

Wilf wrote in the first issue of the combined publication:

The *Country Standard* was first published in 1936 and has continued to be published up to approximately two years ago. The first editor, Jack Dunman [in fact Dunman was not the first editor but had taken the job on in 1946], died in 1974, and I was given the responsibility of keeping the *Country Standard* alive.

We formed a small collective in Norfolk and have, with great fun and many difficulties, kept the journal in production. The loyalty of the readers has maintained our journal, with very interesting letters and very generous contributions to overcome the financial problems.

We have had letters telling us how some readers use the material in the *Standard* when they attend their trades council meetings. Others have told us the *Country Standard* is often used as a basis for a discussion at their local Labour Party meetings. Many elder readers have told us how pleased they are to hear the *Country Standard* falling on their doormats.

Unfortunately a number of the collective have moved from the area, and with the death of some of our colleagues and some getting old, we could not keep the *Country Standard* going at the standard our readers are entitled to. Fortunately we have met a group of people who are prepared to keep it in existence.

Around this time Christina developed cancer of the breast; and then she broke her hip in a fall and was taken to hospital in Norwich. After being transferred to Cromer district hospital she died a couple of weeks later, on 1 September 1997.

The following year Wilf's continued work on behalf of pensioners was praised by Jack Jones, who presented him with a crystal decanter. 'Wilf has been a good old fighter for farm workers and pensioners,' he said. 'He really deserves recognition and is still on the board of the *Anglian Pensioner*.' Further recognition came with a plaque in honour of him and Christina which was unveiled at the Burston Strike School. Wilf died of heart disease in Halsey House on 8 April 2001. His occupation on the death certificate was recorded as 'trade union official (retired)'.

The funeral took place at St Faith's crematorium, at 75 Manor Road, Horsham St Faith, close to where Wilf had gone to school, and on the site of the old workhouse where he had shaken hands with one of the inmates as a child. The service was followed by a memorial meeting at Norwich Labour Club. It started with the socialist anthem, the Internationale. Then two former TGWU general secretaries, Jack Jones and Ron Todd, praised Wilf for his tireless campaigning on behalf of others until the end of his life. 'I was always impressed by his wonderfully simple and clearly stated approach to the problems of people, agricultural workers especially, and pensioners more recently,' said Jack. 'Wilf fought in such a way as to inspire others. He was always on the side of the oppressed and he would want us to carry that support forward in the future. We can celebrate his life by strengthening the struggle.'

Ron added that Wilf had been a staunch champion of the union movement and 'had a feeling of compassion for all workers and their problems'. Long time friend, Mike Ward, also paid a heartfelt tribute: 'He was a big man by stature and big in his presence at any meeting, with an aura of confidence and an unflappable charisma. He was a leader without being bombastic or overbearing, and would always listen to and respect other views. In return, he was respected by other people regardless of their political backgrounds.' Another old friend, Tony Gould, who was a senior regional industrial organiser of the union, added: 'Wilf was a trade unionist to his very fingertips, who did wonderful work for members who needed help, as well as giving inspiration and encouragement to others. You couldn't be in his company for long without realising that he considered himself a citizen of the world.'

Stan Newens (retired Labour MP for Epping) recalled the time when Wilf was fighting the eviction of farm worker Chris Morris and his four children. 'Wilf was indefatigable,' he said, 'with his vision of a caring and sharing society in the interest of all humanity, for which we must carry on the struggle.' Francis Beckett said that Wilf was 'a man of principle and integrity, but not austere'. However violently he was attacked in the press (for supporting land nationalisation for example), he always 'treated his critics with kindness and respect, as he did all his political opponents.' Chris Kaufman added that 'when he was frozen out of the union and jobs for being a communist he refused to change his politics to advance his position. He was not rigid, because he wanted to involve people and reach out for broad alliances. Like Nelson Mandela he had a passion for justice for the dispossessed and exploited. I say he gargled with marbles.'

Norwich MP Ian Gibson said that Wilf turned up 'like a magician whenever there was a struggle'. When he had been a member of the International Socialists (forerunner of the Socialist Workers' Party), he recalled, he was involved in an occupation of an old people's home in the 1980s to prevent its closure from lack of funds. 'Wilf was there within a couple of hours and was truly inspirational, keeping us going through despairing times,' he said. He also knew when discretion was the better part of valour. 'We picketed the opening of this very club (Norwich Labour Club) by Harold Wilson as a protest against his support of the Vietnam war,' said Ian. 'I was all for getting stuck in, but Wilf held me back while Gerald Kaufman offered to duff me up.'

After Ewan MacColl's 'The Shoals of Herring' and Paul Robeson's 'Old Man River' (which Wilf always played at his musical nights on Tuesday evenings) had been played, the service ended with a rousing rendition of 'Keep Right on to the End of the Road', led by Jack Jones.

In a House of Commons debate about Norfolk farming on 22 October 2002, Ian Gibson paid a further tribute to Wilf, which was recorded for posterity in *Hansard*.

Wilf and his comrades had 'fought hard to defeat the tied cottage and poor wage system,' he said. 'We should pay tribute to them for establishing that great tradition in Norfolk agriculture. The rich history of struggle against poverty remains part of their culture.'

A fitting epitaph indeed.

Bibliography

Joseph Arch, *Joseph Arch: The Autobiography of Joseph Arch* (MacGibbon & Kee, 1966)

Francis Beckett, *Enemy Within, The Rise and Fall of the British Communist Party* (John Murray, 1995)

Pamela Brooks, *Norwich: Stories of a City* (Fort Publishing, 2003)

G.D.J. Cole and Raymond Postgate, *The Common People, 1746-1946* (University Paperbacks, 1963)

Andrew Collins, *Billy Bragg, Still Suitable for Miners* (Virgin Books, 2007)

R.B. Dobson (ed), *The Peasants' Revolt* (Macmillan Press, 1983)

Alastair Dunn, *The Peasants' Revolt, England's failed revolution of 1381* (Tempus, 2004)

George Edwards, *From Crow-Scaring to Westminster, the autobiography of George Edwards* (reprinted by Larks Press, 2008)

Stella Evans, 'The life and death of Richard Nockolds, hand loom weaver of Norwich', in Michael Holland (ed), *Swing Unmasked: The Agricultural Riots of 1830 to 1832 and their Wider Implications* (Family & Community Historical Research Society Publications, 2005)

Reg Groves, *Sharpen the Sickle! The history of the farm workers' union* (Porcupine Press, 1949; Merlin Press, 1981)

Adrian and Anne Hoare, *On the Trail of Robert Kett of Wymondham* (Wymondham Heritage Society, 1996)

Michael Holland (ed), *Swing Unmasked: The Agricultural Riots of 1830 to 1832 and their Wider Implications* (Family & Community Historical Research Society Publications, 2005)

Pamela Horn, *Joseph Arch, The Farm Workers' Leader* (Roundwood Press, 1971)

Horsham St Faith VC First School, *150th anniversary souvenir booklet*, 2003 (includes Wilf interviews by Hannah Dack, Laura

Summers, William Farrow, Philip Milbourne, and Leanne Tromans)

Kate Hudson, *CND, Now More Than Ever, The Story of a Peace Movement* (Vision Paperbacks, 2005)

Steve Humphries and Pamela Gordon, *A Man's World, From Boyhood to Manhood 1900-1960* (BBC Books, 1996)

Robert Lee, *Unquiet Country, Voices of the Rural Poor, 1820-1880* (Windgather Press, 2005)

Douglas Low, Low's Book (1842)

S.P. Mackenzie, *Politics and Military Morale* (Clarendon Press, 1992)

Frank Meeres, *A History of Norwich* (Phillimore, 1998)

A.L. Morton, *A People's History of England* (Lawrence & Wishart, 1989)

Mark O'Brien, *When Adam delved and Eve span, a history of the Peasants' Revolt of 1381* (New Clarion Press, 2004)

Kristine Mason O'Connor, *Joan Maynard, Passionate Socialist* (Politico's, 2003)

Val Porter, *British Cattle* (Shire Publications, 2001)

Tom Potter, recorded interview, *The Burston Rebellion, The Longest Strike in History* (CD recorded in 1984 by David Holland Sound Recording, re-released 2003)

Bob Scarth, *We'll all be union men, The story of Joseph Arch and his union* (Industrial Pioneer Publications, 1998)

Keith Skipper, *Larn Yarself Norfolk* (Nostalgia Publications, 2005)

E.P. Thompson, *The Making of the English Working Class* (Penguin, 1980)

Trustees of Burston Strike School, *The Burston Strike School* (undated but post-1985)

TUC, *The Tolpuddle Martyrs* (Trades Union Congress, 2000)

William White, *History, Gazetteer and Directory of Norfolk* (self published, Sheffield, 1883)

Bob Wynn, *Skilled At All Trades, The history of the farmworkers' union, 1947-1984* (TGWU/Frontline, 1993)

Angie Zelter and Arya Bhardwaj, *Snowball: The story of a non-violent civil disobedience campaign in Britain* (Ghandi-in-action, India 1991)

Index